AFRICATION

Dr Samuel Artley D.M.D &
Kenneth Oluwole Lewis

ISBN 0-7414-3932-8

Published by:

INFINITY
PUBLISHING.COM

1094 New DeHaven Street, Suite 100
West Conshohocken, PA 19428-2713
Info@buybooksontheweb.com
www.buybooksontheweb.com
Toll-free (877) BUY BOOK
Local Phone (610) 941-9999
Fax (610) 941-9959

Printed in the United States of America

Printed on Recycled Paper

Published February 2008

DEDICATION

This book is dedicated to our grandfathers, Nkrumah, Toure, Keita, Nyerere and the likes of them; they were patriots with vision beyond their times.

Special appreciation, gratitude, and thanks are extended to Duroseme Taylor. Her superior technical and computer skills have helped to bring all our verbal arguments and theories into visual diagrams. Her assistance is greatly appreciated

As she pursues higher education, our support and prayers go with her in whatever she does. Thanks again, Duro.

Thanks to all our friends for all those brainstorming sessions that we so often have; we are sure all readers can relate to that.

Finally, we have to thank our wives, Julie Artley and Jessica Lewis. Their encouragement and support have created the right atmospheric conditions at home, giving us the time and space to write such positive thoughts of ours into this book.

INTRODUCTION

Africa is a continent made up of fifty-three countries; membership to this African club is by geographic location only. Africans living within Africa identify themselves by nationality, while Africans living out of Africa identify themselves as Africans. Is this a Freudian slip, or is there something to this?

It has been thirty, forty, fifty years since independence. The seeds of independence have been sown; the fruits of independence have been harvested. Modern day Africa is the product of this harvest. It is obvious that decisions made in the past did not bear adequate fruit to meet the needs of today's Africans. Unless the present African generation wants to repeat the same mistakes our parents and grandparents made, then it is about time this generation begins to sow the seeds for the future of Africa. Do not underestimate the little contribution you as an individual can give to this greater cause; your time, your moral support, your boots on the ground will at the very least help by keeping the door open to Africation. Collectively, all these efforts will bear fruit, hopefully sooner than later. Our parents had a chance with Nkrumah. They did nothing, and therefore nothing is what Africa has today.

Africa and Africans have been riding for free on the excuse train for a very long while now. Does Africa want to keep on riding for a bit longer? Does Africa ever want to get off this train? Or, best of all, will Africa ever decide at what station she will get off this excuse train going to nowhere?

These are the questions the African mind, African countries, and African leaders must answer; hopefully, in the process of reading this book, the arguments in support of Africation will become clear and obvious.

TABLE OF CONTENTS

Arguments

Sacrifices

Implementation

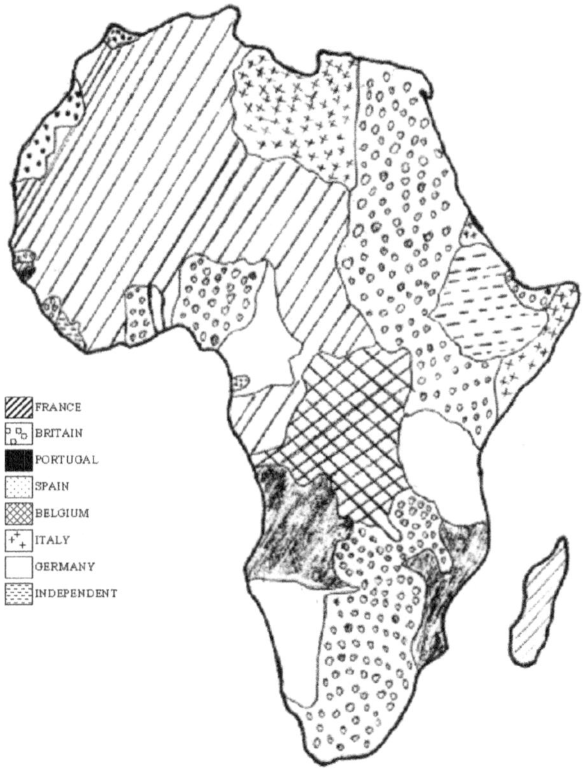

Map showing European claimants to the African continent at the beginning of World War I {1914}

ARGUMENTS

ANATOMY OF THE LAND POST-COLONIAL

To begin with, we will take you back to the basic political map of Africa that we have all come to know so well.

We will have to imagine that the demarcating lines that form the inter-country borders have been temporarily removed, that this mass of land is a single consolidated unit. Put very simply, what you see, is what it is, not those imaginary lines crisscrossing the continent. Upon that note you have to brace yourself and prepare for a dose of reality.

It is no mystery. From tiny Gambia to the vast Congo, we have fifty-three countries functioning more like enclaves than countries, each with its own form of government, ranging from:

- Military régime
- Democratic régime
- Semi-communist régime
- Socialist regime
- Dictatorial regime
- Pro-active religion regime
- Lifetime democratic presidential state

Basically, you name it, most likely it is here in this vast continent of ours.

Every single country has its leader and its agenda. This combination of leader and agenda represents the voice of a nation. These enclaves, collectively put together, result in multiple voices and multiple agendas being pushed at the same time. This is a sure recipe for stagnation and chaos, which is the state of modern day Africa. The result is that no single message or agenda gets put forward or is seen through.

It is therefore imperative that repositioning of the continent be brought about, resulting in a united leadership with a unified voice to set the agenda and thereafter to bring about order instead of thc status quo of chaos. This order will be achieved when we have a unified continent, which will be the motherland, as it implies, for all fifty-three enclaves within the current continent.

Going back into Africa's history pre-European invasion, there were multiple African societies that had histories of success. Those societies had succeeded in terms of stability in leadership as well as economic success. Such societies were Mali and Songhai, Zulu nation, Dahorney Empire, etc.; the list goes on and on.

Yes, it's true all these empires eventually fell. The big difference between the fall of these empires and the preceding was that these fell to the European invasion. Europe immediately introduced fragmentation to the African continent. With the arrival of fragmentation, the natural progression of events regarding the rise and fall of empires was interrupted.

Empires were never allowed to rise or fall. As a matter of fact, the phrase "rise or fall of empires" is expunged from the vocabulary of modern day Africa. With all my readings, I have never come across such phrase used to describe any society within Africa during or post colonial.

Hence, in effect, the partition of Africa had a static effect on the evolution of motherland Africa. Had the partition of Africa never happened, the normal progression there would have been the rise of a stronger and better empire to replace the fallen, just as it was hundreds or thousands of years before.

African nations should take a pause, rethink their situations. Since 1884 (scramble and partition of Africa) up to date, no great kingdom or empire has risen on this vast continent. The most obvious reason for this lack thereof is fragmentation.

Fragmentation had the effect of containing the Leadership within the proverbial containment box drawn or demarcated since 1885.

Given the demarcated landscape that Africa is today, the likes of Sundiata Keita, Mansa Musa, Shaka Zulu, Osman Danfodio, etc., would have never happened. Those leaders would never have made it into the history books as we know of them today.

However, the fragmented status quo will continue to give Africa the likes of Adi Amin, Charles Taylor, civil wars of Sierra Leone, Sudan, etc. One exception to this theory is Nelson Mandela.

Mandela is a great leader. Had he been younger, had the demarcated borders been absent, the greatness of such a leader would not have been contained within the walls of South Africa. Because of the difficult constraints imposed by fragmentation and the age at which he got into power, Mandela, is the Mansa Musa of his time and that of modern day Africa.

Fragmentation did not allow the proverbial vacuum of leadership to form within the motherland. As a result, there are no voids left to be filled by any of the aspiring current leaderships. This void will continue to be absent as long as the status quo fragmented Africa continues.

Unless the containment walls or borders are removed, the plight of motherland Africa will be static. Successive generations will find Africa more difficult than their parents or grandparents. With removal of those demarcating lines, the natural cycle of leadership will be back in motion. Africa can then look forward to the next Mansa Musa, Shaka Zulu, Nelson Mandela and the likes of them.

ANATOMY OF THE LAND PRE-COLONIAL

This is a hypothetical map of ancient Africa; it attempts to show some of the empires or kingdoms that existed way back in the heyday of Africa. All kingdoms were four to six times larger than many countries of modern day Africa. That is the advantage ancient African societies had over fragmented Africa. Because of this size advantage, those societies were able to emerge into stable and prosperous empires as we know of them today.

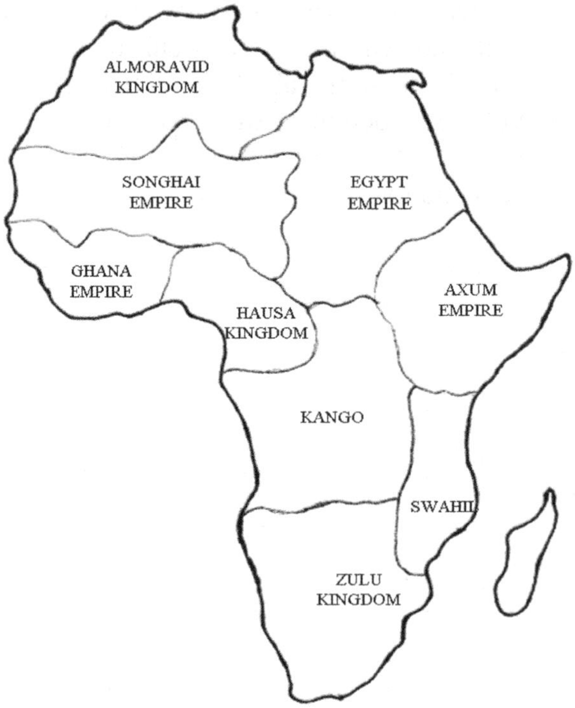

The map shows African societies that existed before the arrival of Europeans into the African continent.

Those societies were very stable; all of them enjoyed many years and generations of stability. Economically, those societies did extremely well for themselves. Those societies for their time had better trading arrangements than today's Africa (21st Century Africa).

Trading then was simple, straightforward, and fair. As a result, all of those societies had positive balances of trade. In modern day Africa, most if not all societies have to contemplate their daily trading transactions with very unfavorable, unfair, and often complicated processes. As a result, all commercial transactions bring additional headaches on top of the usual risk of entrepreneurship.

Looking back to our ancient ancestors, what did they do right?

First: Those societies were geographically viable to begin with. Those societies could support themselves; they had access to all their needs within their territories. All had access to the sea as well as the interior for all their resource needs. Best of all, their territories were so vast that they were practically immune to the modern day famine that so often plagues many African nations.

This resistance was due in part to the natural geographical diversities within all of those societies. However, in modern days, access is there but access is restricted. For some societies, access to god-given oceans is completely denied.

Second: Trade was open. Trade between societies and kingdoms was not regulated or hindered by customs guards and prohibitive legislation. This was fair trade at its best, the likes of which modern day Africa can only dream about.

Finally: There was stability. Such stability lasted for years, in most cases for a generation or more. In other words, the usual instability that modern-day Africa endures was not an issue as it is today.

Africation will seek to take modern day Africa way back into the days preceding 1885. From then on, the search for Africa's independence should begin until a unified Africa becomes a reality.

Therefore, the independence of Africa is directly related to the unification of Africa. These two entities cannot be dealt with separately; viewing these separately will give the perception of false independence, which is the status quo Africa had all these years. Yes, that's right and true for all fifty-three, they have been living off fool's gold.

3

THE AFRICAN EXPECTATIONS

Over the years, through many discussions and debates with my family and friends regarding the plight of Africa, I came to realize that we as Africans have very low expectations. The bar, for most African people, is usually set very low.

Starting out in life with low expectations will eventually lead to low achievements.

At this stage of Africa's development, which is now about 40-50 years since independence, Africa is a mature adult with kids to raise. Our grandparents had great expectations. They expected to achieve independence, and that they did. Our parents had low expectations; they expected to enjoy and perhaps develop their newly found independence, and that they fell short of achieving.

Our generation, as of yet, has not decided what its expectations should be. This is the generation on the verge of finding itself at the control helm; we are about to become the captains of modern day Africa. By no choice of ours, we will have to be in charge. We will have to set the agenda, and finally we will have to set the expectations for the short and long term future of Africa. Ultimately, this generation will have to deliver or fail to deliver their expectations.

Just like the alpha female who leads the wolf pack to the next feeding grounds, so will this alpha generation (i.e. generation in charge) have to lead motherland Africa to the next twenty or thirty years into the future. Will generation alpha have low expectations which will eventually yield low achievements, or will this generation have great expectations which will eventually yield great or greater achievements?

Most in generation alpha are usually very busy. Their daily schedules are fully booked, they barely have enough time for themselves, and their usual day-to-day survival activities are overwhelming. Faced with such busy schedules, this generation does not have the luxury of time to make future expectations for the short and long term future of motherland Africa.

As I tried to explain earlier, this is a role the alpha generation has to assume through no choice of theirs. Such a role they assumed as a result of the natural default of the cycle of life. Our grandparents have died; our parents are dying or about to die. Hence, this generation is about to wake up to the reality of the new role nature has imposed upon them. As of yet, all in this generation are coasting through life. The setting of expectations is not a priority; at the moment, most would like to believe that there is plenty of time to do just that in the future.

Well, there might be lots of time. Our parents had a similar attitude, but the reality on the ground of today's Africa is the result of such attitudes. I would certainly hope this generation does not want to follow in their footsteps.

I propose **Africation** as the ideal expectation for this generation. It is attainable, it is practical, and of course, it is the ultimate expectation.

Until generation alpha breaks away from the culture of low expectations and begins to have great expectations, then and only then will unification of Africa be possible. Africation provides an easy channel and a forum for the overwhelmingly busy generation alpha to participate and shape its future, that of its children and those yet unborn.

MARGINALISATION OF TRIBALISM AND TRIBAL CONFLICT

To be part of a tribe is a fulfillment of one's sense of belonging; those who belong to tribes are the lucky ones.

Hence, this is a heritage that ought to be flaunted. But tribal related conflict should no longer be a gravitating force that continues to keep this great motherland and its people on their knees. Yes, it is true; there are numerous tribes in any given country (enclave).

Within any enclave, one tribe often finds itself as the dominant tribe and therefore sits in a position of power while the minorities are kept out. This practice is nothing new, and it is not likely to come to an end any time soon as long as the status quo continues.

Consider all the enclaves within the motherland today; none so far has succeeded in making affirmative progress toward actually marginalizing the effects of tribal prejudices or biases. To date, any progress has only been in the form of lip service, denouncing tribal biases.

With the consolidation of enclaves and therefore tribal coalition, there lies a true opportunity to immediately neutralize every single tribe regardless of how big, diverse, or entrenched they have become over the years.

This coalition of tribe and enclave leads to African unification, the process of which is **Africation**:

- Under this system no one individual tribe will ever be in a position to be dominant
- No one tribe can set the agenda all by itself, and
- No majority tribe can impose its will upon any minority.

As a result, dominant tribes become marginalized. These marginalized tribes will be forced to form alliances. These alliances will then have to gravitate together to form some sort of political body through which their views will have to be expressed.

Appointment to a position of power will then have to be fulfilled by some other criteria besides tribal connections; thus, this will be a palpable step toward affirmative marginalization of tribal connection as the qualifying factor. Qualified individuals from all tribes will suddenly find themselves being sought after for positions for which they otherwise would not have been considered. Even the mighty, big tribes will be marginalized; these big tribes will have to bring their issues to the table.

There they will have to form alliances with other tribes that have the same political agenda, and this will be the birth of true alliances and cooperation among brothers and sisters of the motherland. Forward movement to a true democracy will begin to crop up; individuals will be judged on their merits and competencies. Incompetent individuals will be dealt the cards they deserve and will not be retained because of their tribal affiliations.

The issue of a dominant language will also find itself as a non-issue. Hence, under these conditions, different tribes will be forced to seek a more common medium of communication acceptable to all tribal clans. Sure enough, the integrity of each tribe at its home base will remain sound and strong.

The plague on Africa, the tower of Babel, will no longer confuse, frustrate, and hinder the future generation. In the event of tribal conflicts, which are bound to crop up at the local level, this time around there will be a consolidated military and police authority that is well equipped, fully trained, and easily deployed to suppress any such conflict before it escalate to the level of Rwanda, etc.

Such forces will no longer be under the control of biased officers, who at one point or another have had direct interest in or connection to either party of the warring tribes. Rwanda-like conflict will never be allowed to fester to the level it got to; timely intervention by the consolidated authorities there and elsewhere will be highly welcomed as a security guarantee.

Thus, marginalization or neutralization of all tribal influence within the continent is imperative, and this can only be achieved by consolidation of the people, consolidation of the brothers, sisters, and nations to form the motherland that Africa truly is.

IVORY-TEE IS AN EXAMPLE OF TRIBAL CONFLICT

Ivory Coast, the words used to describe this enclave in the past, has been a stable, successful role model, and has many other positive developments. Such was the case in the past. Today, none of these is true. It is a simple case of a big mess. This is hard to believe, especially for my generation, which grew up viewing Ivory Coast as a pearl amongst all enclaves within Africa.

The fact is what we have seen happening to Ivory Coast is not an illusion. It is the reality on the ground for the entire west coast of Africa; hence, it is fair to say that as Ivory Coast goes, so does the rest of Africa. No single country is immune from such frequent chaos and destruction.

To understand why Ivory Coast, of all African states, should be falling on the wayside, we must first of all understand how the current point of conflict started in this once very stable and promising enclave within the motherland.

The word **ivory-tee** we have all seen or heard in every single enclave within this Africa. Ivory-tee means born and raised in Ivory Coast. Anything short of that is not acceptable; if someone born in Ghana, Guinea, or any other sister land is then raised in Ivory Coast from day 2 after birth, he or she is still not acceptable as an Ivorian.

Ivory-tee, therefore, is a camouflage. Its true meaning is an expansion of tribal interest and conflicts that always seek to suppress anyone outside of the main tribe from excelling.

The end result is the usual military mess that Africa has become very familiar with.

Hence, very simply, if chaos and instability are happening to the once-stable Ivory Coast, then why should they not happen to Gambia, Ghana, Nigeria, Kenya, Uganda, Rwanda, etc., down the line to all fifty-three sister states? It is only a matter of time; in fact, a good majority of these sister lands has already experienced chaos. Unfortunately, looking ahead, I see no reason why repeated episodes of chaos and instability will stop happening, again and again, throughout the entire African landscape.

The bottom line is that Africa has to wake up and realize that the system was designed to do what it is doing now, which is to fail. Africa is on an automatic fail cycle. The collective society lacks a fail-safe mechanism. This cycle cannot be stopped by foreign aid, coups d'état, newly-discovered liquid or solid gold, or even by the propping military presences of the supreme colonial masters.

This cycle can and will only be stopped and redirected into a fail-safe system via unification.

Under unification, the phrase "fail proof" could be used to describe the functioning mechanism of the motherland. Under unification, the entire continent will not be held captive by some foolish tribal squabble within the western, northern, or any other part of the continent. There will always be cooler heads to prevail over whatever tribal or regional conflict arises. Under Africation, these areas of conflict will now have the entire continent to contend with, not just another minority tribe or government to contend with.

Africation is a must. Until that is achieved, the status quo of the automatic fail cycle will continue to roll.

The flawed design in the African society is the unnatural, fragmented state imposed upon her. This unnatural impediment has to be removed to overhaul the system.

Using Ivory Coast as the poster child, how would potential conflict have been resolved under the current status quo as opposed to under a unified motherland?

Under the status quo, these are the options. Groups or individuals facing an ivory-tee-like scenario will have to resort to:

(a) A leader in a position of power who can and will most likely exclude any opposition he/she chooses to exclude from the political, economic, or social systems under his/her control.

(b) Excluded opposition usually has no higher mediating authority to resort to, they are therefore forced into one of these options:

  (i) Go back to home base, rally up friends and family, and organize a small, militant opposition, which is the usual obvious recipe for a chaos.

  (ii) Go back to home base and pray for divine intervention, which is what most of our parents did; i.e., the failed generation has been doing this all along. The result here I will refrain from simplifying lest I be accused of being in collusion with satanic or non-religious beliefs. Hence, I would prefer you to make your own conclusion.

On the flipside, assuming the system is overhauled and unification (United Nations of Africa) is achieved, such conflict would have been resolved by the following:

(a) Leaders in power can only suppress opposition at the local level. Such opposition has the opportunity to take the conflict to a totally neutral, external, higher and mediating authority that is far removed from the point of conflict. Under such a scenario, at least a fair and reasonable compromise will be arrived at.

(b) After a reasonable compromise is reached, if one or more of the parties involved do not intend to abide by the agreement, there will always be a prevailing high authority with lots of united muscles to enforce the will of the motherland. Extremist or militant groups or governments will be isolated, contained, and sanitized appropriately to an acceptable level by the consolidated authority.

Hence, the cycle of military mess that plagues motherland Africa today will at least be contained. The mess in Ivory Coast would have been stopped before it started, or at least would have been contained. It would have been described as just a civil unrest as opposed to the reality that it is: a big mess.

What a waste; what a pity. This conflict, we all know, started over a problem that should have never been a problem or a potential problem: But for the flawed African design. Ivorians born and raised in Ivory Coast were denouncing the citizenship of other Ivorians simply because a parent is not a born Ivorian.

This is very counterproductive and counter progressive. Such thoughts would be rendered mute, and therefore, such thoughts would not have been entertained under a unified continent. However, under the current status quo of multiple states and countries, all sorts of excuses are used by large tribal groups even if the excuse does not make sense. These excuses are used to incite and attempt to exclude legitimate and competent leaders from the political system.

In the case of Ivory Coast and the rest of the sister enclave of Africa, to use such lame reasons to slash and burn the entire motherland is nothing but tribalism in camouflage.

6

AFRICA AND ITS INDEPENDENT DEMOCRACIES

Today, every single enclave within this beloved continent is independent. Most attempts to be democratic, but this concept of independence is a fallacy. The fact is if one looks around motherland Africa, the conclusion is that there is only one game in town; the rules of the game are set by external nationals, or should we say the G8.

Any smart nation that is truly interested in economic empowerment has to play by the rules. For those nations that want to continue the status quo, they better keep their blinders on and make believe they are in lala-land, where there are many games in town and all is hunky-dory.

The fallacy that Africa has its own form of independent democratic republic should be rejected because that is a misnomer, though it is what the phrase describes. The product of these African experiments, as we have seen, is economic dependency on foreign aid, stagnation, and at times, being an outpost for the foreign policies of extra-African nations. Therefore, it is high time this romantic view is buried and the facts on the ground be accepted as they are. That is, independence in the absence of unification is an illusion. Like all illusions, they look great from a distance, but as the years roll by, the painful reality sets in.

African states must play by the rules of the game or they will be punished by the rules of the game. As we all know, there is a big penalty for not playing the game right. This penalty is devaluation, which is administered by the economic enforcement wing of the G8 (that is, the IMF).

It does not matter how isolated or delusional any of our arrogant leaders are. The fact is, a nation's value (currency) will be devalued appropriately to match the degree of deviation a nation has taken from the rule of the day.

Look around. It is obvious that most of our independent democracies are made to dance accordingly to the whipping lashes of the IMF; this surely is not independence. Perhaps it is guided independence, but it is not the real thing.

With consolidation, the motherland does not need external guidance. The principle of self-reliance in her will be a rehearsal exercise. The ultimate goal is absolute independence, sustainable under total isolation.

Though isolation is not what the motherland seeks, in theory and in practical reality, a consolidated motherland should be able to sustain itself in the event of external sanctions or isolation.

NOSTALGIA FOR EARLY POST-COLONIAL DAYS

I was not around for colonial days or the end of colonial days, but I am around during post-colonial times. The legacy of colonial times was obvious during my childhood days. The very few details I can remember from that time were, running around barefooted, kicking ball, the usual boyish adventures and the occasional trouble here and there.

Besides the social activities that are still prevalent (thank God for that), the social culture was good and is still good. Other detail landmarks I have searched hard for, but could only find with much rarity in today's West Africa. Such rare landmarks are:

- Public workers in uniform cleaning the streets and gutters.
- The usual trash trucks collecting trash daily.
- Designated trash collection areas for every neighborhood.
- Public workers and their traffic cones repairing and painting lines on the street,
- Traffic policemen. They are the most obvious absentees; traffic control policemen were always an amusement. I never fully understood their purpose at the time. Now, as an adult, their purpose and value is fully appreciated. Perhaps their value should be more appreciated now than ever before because of major

> changes on the ground, such as population increases, increased migration of rural citizens into the metropolitan areas, more affluent people have access to automobiles, the volume of people on foot has quadrupled, and the usual assistant at the corner shop has been steadily increasing. All these dynamic factors put together end up clogging the streets.

The streets were not designed for such a volume of traffic, both vehicle and pedestrian. To make matters worse, these roads have been left to the elements of nature. The sidewalks were never there, and they are still not there. Pedestrians are therefore forced to share the roads with vehicles.

The roads are heavily infested with potholes, and their conditions are grim. On a total comparison with my childhood days, i.e., the immediate post-colonial period, the public conditions then were much better than they are today. On the positive side, the people in their own private homes have shown remarkable improvements. The houses within those gates are now quite modern, well built, much more personalized, and well constructed. The care for these personal properties is right about where it should be. On the other hand, take two steps out of those gated yards, and the grim reality sets in.

These deficiencies in public conditions might not be noticeable by the people on the ground, simply because the people have become desensitized and have progressed through the natural course of events by adapting and working around whatever conditions they are presented with.

On the grand scale of things, these conditions viewed from outside the box are very discouraging. They project an image of hopelessness; most of all, such conditions are not motivating incentives for external third parties to either invest or infuse any substantial form of capital into such a grim condition.

Most of these conditions are local; any attempt to propose a remedy here will be a deviation from the matter at hand that is being discussed. Africans have to set priorities. At this stage of the continent's development, the most pressing issue is Africation, which is more of a general African problem with a potential impact on the quality of life for all Africans.

Nostalgia for early post-colonial days is seen and felt all over modern day Africa. A very common denominator affecting every living soul on continental Africa is money. From the farmer in the village to the teacher at the high school, the rich businessman up the hill to the ubiquitous beggars at the corners of the streets, all these folks have a realistic understanding of the steady decline the value of their currencies has been undergoing. Concerned or not, these folks are forced to take note as their ability to purchase the daily essentials of life becomes more and more difficult with each passing year, in some cases, each passing month.

To those young readers, most will be surprised to realize that, immediately following independence, many African nations had the value of their currencies tag directly onto the value of the US dollar or French CFA. Yes, at that time, it was a 1:1 relationship. For example:

1 pound Gambia = 1 British pound

1 Cedi Ghana = 1 us dollar

0.60 Naira Nigeria = 1 us dollar

1 CFA Ivory Coast = 1 French franc

1 CFA Senegal = 1 French franc

However, such is not the case in modern day Africa. The value of all currencies has been diminishing. This trend will most likely stay on course through our lifetimes and into the lifetimes of all African children unborn. At the moment, I see no reason for a potential halt or reversal in the current trend.

As Africans, we have bought into the belief that the future cannot be predicted. A good part of that belief might be true; myself being religious, I do agree that the future is in God's hands, but at the same time, there is that small part of African future that could be controlled or at least guided. This is the part of motherland Africa's future that the people have to take control of. This control will only be possible under Africation.

At this stage, Africa should not be having nostalgia; collectively, Africa should be looking into the immediate future, not as to what she can do or is capable of doing, but as to when will unification become a reality? Will the people of Africa help by pushing their local governments into taking the faithful leap into Africation, or will the people of Africa continue to do the usual, which is to stand by and watch while they hope for divine intervention?

I certainly hope not. This generation alpha, I believe, has a better understanding of history than the previous generation. This generation also has the luxury of learning from the mistakes of the previous generation. Besides, I believe that Africation is a natural and a necessary process; we all know nature cannot be cheated or ignored forever. Africation, therefore, is bound to happen. It is only a matter of when, hopefully this generation will realize the urgency of this matter and therefore begin to lay down the foundation, by building global African pressure groups, whose sole function is to bring about African unification at a realistic date in the near future.

MULTIPLICATION AND REDUPLICATION OF PROBLEMS

Life is energy source; energy is finite. Since energy is finite, it is obvious that this energy should be used sparingly and wisely. This is not the case for the status quo in the fifty-three enclaves that Africa is today. The usual day-to-day problems that any collective society has to grapple with are usually multiplied by fifty-three all across this mighty continent of Africa.

- Fifty-three times, the same problems have to be dealt with.
- Fifty-three times, a solution has to be thought of.
- Fifty-three times, the wheel has to be invented to solve the same problem. Hence, fifty-three times, an attempt has to be made to solve the same problem.
- Fifty-three times, limited, scarce resources, both in cash or kind, have to be expended on the same problem.
- Fifty-three times, limited time has to be expended.

We can go on and on, but whichever way one slices or dices it, the common fact remains the same: every single problem has to be multiplied by fifty-three.

This approach to life is very taxing on the people, on the economy, on the natural resources, and on personal or family time. As a result of such repetition, by the end of any given day, only a few resources would be left to conduct or solve other problems. The same thing applies to time left for innovation.

In effect, the net result of problem multiplication and reduplication is to continue failing, thereby maintaining all fifty-three sister countries in a revolving door of everlasting problems.

Africation, on the other hand, unifies the people into one big problem. It is much easier to suffer once and solve that one big problem once, as opposed to solving fifty-three little problems. We all know the big secret about problems. They are here to stay. They never seem to end, so why multiply them unnecessarily?

9

FOREIGN AID, OR THE FORBIDDEN FRUIT

This is the type of aid that has to be taken with a grain of salt. First, one has to understand what foreign aid is all about to the donor nation.

First, it satisfies their altruistic needs. Second, it gives the feel-good effect (esteem needs). This is the most important and exploited component of foreign aid in today's age of global telecommunication. By granting a drop of foreign aid here and there, the donor nation acquires a feel-good effect in the process. This feel-good effect is quickly disseminated from the actions of the government down the ranks to the local citizens of the donor nation. Individual citizens from these nations will jump at the opportunity to toot their horns about their participation in feeding such and such a country. This simple act of humanitarianism is then used as a rod to constantly beat, brand, or glaze the perception that the recipient is in the position of constant need. From then on, the recipient nation has taken the forbidden fruit, to which there are consequences. These consequences are:

Loss of group pride;

Loss of bargaining power; and

Loss of respect.

Recipients of this aid will be reminded of it often, and worst of all, consumption of foreign aid is in itself a suppressant of innovation.

LOSS OF GROUP PRIDE: Regardless of how powerful or respected our individual heads of state and their representatives have become, when these African leaders have to face their colleagues from donor nations, from their body language, an observant viewer will see a humble leader, a pacified and tamed leader. This attitude will trickle down the rank and file to the citizens of the recipient nation.

Africans know a lot about pride. Our parents, particularly our fathers, are full of pride. Pride, to an African man, is that which holds a man together. Yes, our African dads have lots of pride; they are always there for their families. Pride, therefore, is absolutely important to the psyche of all Africans. This pride in itself is what we have at home and lack in the global arena.

An African dad who, under normal healthy conditions, is incapable of providing for his family will face his colleagues with loss of pride; the same applies to our leaders when they have to participate in the global arena shortly after receiving the forbidden fruit or are about to receive foreign aid. By taking the forbidden fruit, these leaders have become co-opted; hence, these leaders will tell the world otherwise, but their actions are not independent. In fact, their actions are coerced, and the perception or lack of independence remains.

These are leaders lead by foreign leaders, and therefore, they are leaders lacking in pride. To all reasonably-minded brothers and sisters of the motherland, it is up to you to help bring pride to our leaders. This, in turn, will disseminate down the rank and file to all brothers and sisters of the land. Pride will only come when our leaders can truly represent the people's interest independently of external influence. Africation will bring African pride back to life.

LOSS OF BARGAINING POWER: This speaks for itself. Once Africa has taken the forbidden fruits or aid, she has sold her soul to the devil (may I clarify, I do not mean to say that the donor nations are the devil). This is because sooner or later it will be time for the recipient nation to pay up to the donor.

Foreign aid might taste good while it is being consumed, but it will sooner run out, leaving a bad taste in the mouth. African leaders have to realize that in this world, only air is free; nothing else is free. Though the perception is that we are receiving free foreign aid, the reality is that this aid has to be paid for, be it in the expectation of your vote on global issues at the United Nations, or be it in shaping national behaviors to suit and accommodate the interest of donor nations. The expectations go on and on.

Looking back at that free foreign aid, it is always a wise investment on the part of the donor nation, because the recipient will always have to pay back in cash or in kind. Cash, we all know, is not possible; kind is, however, quite possible. Therefore, kind it will always be.

Reasonably-minded brothers and sisters, it is up to you to consolidate and create alternatives within this vast land of ours, to meet our needs and close the voids that would otherwise be plugged with the forbidden fruit (foreign aid).

LOSS OF RESPECT: this is not obvious; it is the subliminal result of taking the forbidden fruit. To see this loss of respect, one has to view the African-donor relationship by stepping out of the box (i.e., view it from outside the motherland). This will be seen in the perceptions created within the telecommunication media of the donor nations. Mass media in these donor nations constantly projects and emphasizes the worst parts of the African enclave.

All over the motherland, there are enclaves of absolute poverty. Even among the most prosperous African nations, this absolute poverty, desperation, and hopelessness of the African plight is often paraded on the mainstream media of these donor nations. As a result, this message is constantly imprinted in the mind of the donor nation's audience. This audience, in turn, develops a negative perception of Africa;

since half of life is perception, that perception often translates into respect or disrespect.

A long term effect of being a recipient is lack of respect for the recipient nation, and so it goes for the rest of Africa.

For those Africans who cannot envision a consolidated Africa, well, they don't have to search too far into their dreams and memory. When it comes to negative perception, the continent is already collectively packaged as a unified block of negative mess. Positive developments and incidences are always categorized in small, isolated packages. The old cliché, "good things come in small packages," truly applies here.

This goes back to the concept of built-in design flaws of the African continent. Positive traits cannot be viewed or perceived as unified traits. Positive traits are traits to be credited to individual nations, just as the system is designed to do (containment). On the other hand, since the media unifies and condemns all of Africa for negative traits via perception, it is much easier to remember one big negative perception than multiple minor positive perceptions.

Reasonably-minded brothers and sisters, if Africa is perceived negatively as a unified group, then why not unify and create a unified perception for both the negatives and the positives?

Foreign aid, in its current form of drip, drip, drip, does more good for the donor nation than it does for the recipient nation. Foreign aid in the marshal plan form is the only form of forbidden fruit that is worth the trouble; anything short of a marshal plan is just a spinning of wheels, i.e., lots of energy wasted, but no significant achievements.

For those diehard brothers, sisters, leaders, and countries addicted to foreign aid, start thinking hard, because the foreign aid spigots (funds) are shrinking. With the recent repositioning of Europe as the EU, aid is not coming Africa's way any time soon. All excess funds of meaningful value will be going to the new members, to prop up their economies and bring them up to the European economic standard.

These merging nations will sooner emerge into shiny cities, once again leaving Africa in the dust, with each enclave still fending for itself, while all fifty three states continues to bask in the illusion of being an independent country.

10

DON'T BLAME THE GOVERNMENT – IT'S THE DESIGN THAT IS FLAWED

Imagine if Africa, since its conception into a multi-state venture, were a corporation. Each state is a department within the corporation, starting from Angola, Algeria, etc., all the way to Zaire. After more than thirty years of not making profit, or at least being able to hold its own, in the normal cause of events such a business would have been dissolved—unless daddy got some money and is propping up the company. Such is the case in Africa today. It is being propped up by foreign aid. This commercial venture of multi-state Africa has failed to yield a profit, so we must therefore start to consider its dissolution from the current status quo.

Governmental institutions, particularly the ruling central governments, have been cited, blamed, and held responsible for African failure; others have blamed the people collectively for being corrupt. I refuse to believe it is the corruption, because corruption has been with mankind since the beginning of time. Globally, every society has its corrupt members, yet most of these societies have become profitable ventures; the overwhelming failed venture resides within the continent of Africa.

The blame on the government is overstated. Again, I will attempt to make this point with another business model.

An African state today is like a businessman (entrepreneur) who goes out to shop for a location to set up his business. He eventually settles for a back road location, because the rent is cheap. His business idea is great; he is definitely not lacking in his idea. But he begins to wonder why the business is not bringing in as much revenue as he had projected. At that point, he starts to blame the economy or the people, of course forgetting about his choice of location. Such is the case with African states today,

At first glance, it seems that poor governments are the problems, when in reality; poor governments are responsible for only one-tenth of her problems. The remaining nine-tenths of the reason for the lackadaisical performance of all African enclaves globally are in its inherent design flaw. Basically, the individual states are performing exactly as they were designed to perform, that is, to fail. They will continue to fail until the overall design is changed, rearranged, and overhauled.

Africation provides an opportunity to change such a flawed system into a practical and viable system. By failed design or flawed design, we go back to the partition and fragmentation of the continent in 1885 into multiple weaker and unsustainable little enclaves called countries, pulling the continent and its people in all directions. A great number of African nations are too small to be geographically viable by themselves; others are geographically landlocked. Being landlocked by nature is an unnatural predicament for any nation.

This map shows the unnatural, fragmented state of modern day Africa. In the normal course of events, a great number of these countries would have been part of greater empires or kingdoms, just as it has always been pre-1885.

At the end of the days, years, and generations, the result is chaos. Wasn't it Julius Caesar who said divide and conquer? But in today's politically correct societies, a flawed design is an acceptable status quo as long as that design flaw does not affect the interest of the designers (i.e., colonial nations).

Redesigning and correcting all the design flaws of the continent will have to come under the umbrella of unification and centralization of whatever resources are left. It is only when the continent and her people converge to move in a single direction that the great march forward will begin. Anything else, regardless of how successful and isolated an enclave or country is, such success is temporal, because the plug could be pulled at any time by only one or two opposing forces that are mostly from outside the continent. This inability for any African state to sustain itself in the absence of external influences will always bring into question the independence of any African country.

DON'T BLAME THE GOVERNMENTS – IT'S THE FAILURE OF THE PEOPLE TO PARTICIPATE

For once, let us not blame our various governments. The captain of the Bismarck was not blamed for the loss of the ship. The African system of fragmented enclaves, now called countries, was doomed to fail from the inception, and it will continue to fail until the system is corrected. As of now, let us spare the leaders, spare them the blame, regardless of how corrupt or unscrupulous they are. After all, the problem is far bigger than any one of them.

From what we have seen in the past and as of now, it does not matter how smart, dedicated, or honest these African leaders in the governments are, because the decks are fully stacked against them. After all, fragmentation of Africa did happen, and it happened for a reason; this is where the blame should lie. The restrictive effects of fragmentation are what the whole continent of Africa is failing to realize or is opting to ignore. Not until the countries and the people realize that the fragmented geographical state in which the motherland has been is a structurally flawed system, only then will we start to alleviate and remedy some of our systematic pathologies, or at least be in a position to solve our own problems. A family that can solve its own problems will be able to speak for itself and therefore have control over itself. Africation will transform the motherland into a strong family of African nations.

Most African governments have very good intentions for their people, but for some reason, they usually lose the drive and oomph to implement their intentions. Thus, they usually end up being sidetracked into the infinite hall of ever-present underachievers. At this point, we must start to question ourselves. Why do all these leaders start out with good intentions, but end up in the same predicament of underachieving? After all, they are from different regions, from different cultures and school of thought, and they range from all ages and generations.

- Perhaps we ought to take a closer look at the people these leaders are leading.
- Perhaps these leaders have been boxed into a losing corner by their own people by accepting anything with no questions asked.
- Perhaps the decks are fully stacked against the African people because of the inherent design flaw.
- Perhaps these leaders do not have an active or participating flock that constantly demand their attentions.
- Perhaps the failure of the flock to interact with these leaders has led to the nonchalant and disconnected attitude that these leaders eventually develop.

This failure of the flock to interact with its leaders is seen all across the board in Africa in the form of failure to peacefully protest or challenge authority when it sees fit. Most, if not all, of our folks believe that authorities should not be challenged under any circumstances, that challenge to authority is futile, and that challenging authority is also a form of hooliganism. Hooliganism, from an African mom or dad's point of view, is a disgrace. We all know what is next. An African family has no room to accommodate disgrace.

Far too often, brothers and sisters of the beloved motherland hesitate to peacefully protest or voice out their concerns in a timely manner, when words or a simple act of peaceful protest would remedy the situation. They will instead sit idly by and watch the situation get out of hand. At this point, the situation will violently explode into another of our many deadly revolutions or coup d'etat.

Failure of the flock to express its dissatisfaction is always justified by the fear of the potential consequences that some ruthless leader will inflict upon its people. The flock that has fear of potential consequences is the same flock who claims that foreign powers are responsible for the continued suppression of our motherland and her economy. Such arguments are illusions, and diversionary tactics to shift the blame away from the self. These illusions are temporal. Reality always has a way of catching up with flocks that have failed to interact with their leaders, or have allowed their leader to ride on free passes.

A desert fox that quenches its thirst through a mirage will be chasing an illusion; sooner or later, it will have to face a crisis. Such is the fate of our people. We often believe and like to believe that it is only our neighbors, distantly removed villages, and those in the governments that are affected. If only we stay in our little happy corner, then all will be fine at home. After all, most of us are nobodies; we are not part of the political administrative bodies, we are simply minding our little business at home. Hell no! It isn't so simple.

Like the desert fox chasing a mirage, the people of Africa are busy chasing an illusion. Eventually, sooner more often than later, we seem to find our 'nobody-selves' minding our own business at our happy little homes, stuck in a permanent state of crisis. Then who do we go on to blame? The usual, of course—(1) our governments, and (2) foreign governments.

Well, we can continue to chase an illusion, or wake up and search for an oasis. This I will leave to your imagination, but it is definitely not the fault of our corrupt governments. Yes, that is right; it is not the fault of the governments. They are doing the best they can with a faulty design.

Africation will remove the flaw in the design, thus bringing the governments and their people together. The people under Africation will have to interact with their governments; the balance of power will switch to the people, and the people will then have higher expectations for which they will hold their leaders accountable.

12

INABILITY TO RESPOND TO DISTRESS

Africa is a continent of proverbs; despite all the overstated differences among Africans, from the Arab Africans, Black Africans, Indian Africans, White Africans, and all others, one constant that is prevalent in all African cultures is our passion for proverbs. On graduation day, I picked up my diploma from one of the very big universities in the city of brotherly love (Philadelphia). As usual, there were many speeches given on the podium; it was like every other graduation, a long day of speeches, full of advice from all those old men and women. One professor's speech got my attention. He quoted a proverb from Africa; it goes: "pick a twig, everybody can snap it, but pick up a few and put them together, and not everybody can snap this." Draw your own conclusion from this proverb; these are strong words of wisdom from Africa to the rest of the world, but to Africa, these words seem to lose their weight. They are just out there with no meaningful impact on the reality of life for all Africans.

Individual countries are single twigs, but collectively they form a bundle of twigs, which can withstand a lot. Natural disasters, be it flood or drought, are part of nature; they are here to stay, and it is just a matter of time before we will all get our fair share of these. The motherland is somewhat fortunate, because most other parts of the world have it worse than Africa. Typhoons, volcanoes, earthquakes, hurricanes, etc., do not often visit Africa. Still, when it is Africa's turn to get its share of natural disasters, we are always caught in the same hopeless position we were the last time around, simply stuck in hopeless mode.

Every tiny and large country within the continent is waiting on each other or lacks the collective strength to move and shake things up. This inability to respond to stimuli is an unnatural behavior; living things have to respond to stimuli. If our current, fragmented states or independent countries cannot respond to stimuli, then perhaps we need to take a closer look at the system. It might be in need of revamping.

The system as it is right now lacks the ability to respond to natural disasters, when floods or draughts strike. A big nothing happens. There is no social or organized body in place to handle and manage these problems. Hence, the system has broken down and it needs fixing.

The disaster of current times in Africa is HIV/AIDS. The ability to fight disease in Africa, especially HIV/AIDS, is grim. Still, Africa is critical of developed countries when they fail to make their AIDS pharmaceuticals available. These developed nations are simply acting in a selfish manner, securing their own group's interest. In the same manner, we as Africans are selfish, too. We are stuck in an illusion, hoping that our problems will go away before they get to us; meanwhile, we do a big nothing to help our societies. We are therefore in no position to criticize or even ask for help. After all, you've got to help yourself before you can be helped.

Africa needs to wake up from its sleep. The problems that Africa has are bigger than any foreign aid or natural disaster has been. Today, the motherland is sick. HIV/AIDS is ravaging its children. In the midst of this catastrophe, somehow the system is recognizing its inherent flawed design. In its effort to battle AIDS, the fragmented states have finally decided to pool their resources, some pledging 15% of their GDP toward research for battling AIDS. Though this is a progressive effort, it is much too little to help with a remedy for the sickness of the motherland. This is simply because the consolidated 15% GDP going towards AIDS research will end up in the medical schools and research institutes of the greater world.

This great AIDS war for Africa adversely affects two of her precious resources:

(1) **People** in terms of loss of life. This is the part of the equation that the motherland has sacrificed African youths in great numbers by the millions.

(2) **Intellectual rights**, or shall we say intellectual property. This is the part that will most likely be the property of all but the motherland. Though the motherland will lose a great number of her children to HIV/AIDS, all those losses will be in vain, simply because the motherland is not in the position to consolidate the research or knowledge gained. This inability to consolidate knowledge within the motherland will result in this knowledge being consolidated elsewhere. There goes the intellectual property right again.

With Africation, a roundup of the best scientific minds is possible; the best schools in the land will be used, and of course that 15% GDP will not only be spent within the continental motherland. It will also keep the societies of scientists well paid and proud of their jobs, as well as keep them prepare for that battle of tomorrow, which Africa will have to fight again and again—not with tanks and antitank weapons, but with anti-microbials and pharmaceuticals.

By then, the residual effect of intellectual property rights, of course, will lie within the motherland. Retaining such property rights will produce a much greater return than any current individual government can promise or any foreign aid will satisfy.

Yes, if Africa sees the benefit of consolidating 15% GDP, surely there will be an even greater benefit under the consolidation of 100% GDP. That is Africation.

Africa does not need to wait for a combo disease (combination disease) such as AIDS plus XX (diseases that are yet to be named) before she starts to move to 100% GDP consolidation.

Though HIV/AIDS spells disaster and gloom for Africa, a lot of good has come out of this disaster that would benefit the long-term interests of the motherland, especially when she decides to consolidate. Such benefits are:

(1) First of all, it brings to light the need for open communication about the most taboo topics, sex and its ramifications. In the process, this has helped to set up efficient communication methods and channels. However rudimentary the methods are, the presence of HIV/AIDS has brought this link into existence.

(2) Though the remedy for AIDS is a work in progress, the difficulties and challenges posed by the disease have shown the value of consolidating resources, at least financial recourses, toward battling a common menace or enemy.

On the flipside, as of today, I could not recall any academic institute within the motherland that could represent her with a commanding degree of respect in any worldwide gathering of research scientists or institutions. In this world of pure science, capability is important and good, but results are respected in the absolute with no consideration of borders or racial orientation.

Though Africa has many highly qualified and competent scientists within the continent itself, these scientists work mostly in small enclaves, working in total isolation from other scientists within the neighboring enclaves. Obviously, capability is not lacking, but result is lacking.

The obvious consequence of the dispersal of capable or qualified scientists, coupled with the usual argument of lack of funds, is the lack of tangible results. This translates to the rest of the world as a lack of respect for those great minds within the continent. Results, as I said earlier, are absolute in the scientific world.

That usual scapegoat punch line that Africa uses (lack of funds) is an old and obsolete argument. Perhaps Gambia, Mali, Senegal, Nigeria, or Ghana can make that argument individually, but Africa as a whole, with its 850 million people or more, should definitely not make such an argument. Therefore, with consolidation and pooling of resources, the motherland will be able to muster enough resources to fully fund one institute that will not only be actively involved in the battle for AIDS and other diseases, but will also be a leader in the field of science that all upcoming scientists within Africa, from every little facet or enclave, can aspire toward.

The system as it is today, makes it is impossible for local scientists or pharmacists to come up with any new drug or drugs. Even with the local herbal drugs, used since the days of our grandparents, Africa is finding it cannot claim such herbs as its own any longer; these herbal recipes are finding themselves out of the continent, and are quickly claimed as intellectual property of modern day pharmaceutical companies worldwide.

Africa then turns around and criticizes these companies for not sharing the profits with her or donating some of the drugs back to her. Once again, Africa can only blame its continued decision to stay the course and keep the status quo of fragmented states for its current position.

This status quo is not conducive to the breeding of large-scale pharmaceutical companies that are capable of packaging and branding grandma's herbal drug recipes as their own. Existing pharmaceutical companies lacks the capability, both in market and financial share, to globally stand by their products and make legal challenges where they see fit. Instead, the status quo only encourages the breeding of small pharmaceutical companies here and there, with hardly enough funds to duplicate basic antibiotics.

The lack of a controlling pharmaceutical body within the motherland is a prevailing disaster. This will continue to be the case under the status quo. The fact on the ground, as of now, is that there is no universally accepted standard for pharmaceutical drugs throughout the continent. Unfortunately, pharmaceuticals happen to be the only commodity that can cross multiple customs and military borders with ease.

These small, antibiotic-duplicating factories, scattered all across the motherland, often fiddle with the concentration of their products to maximize profit. These unscrupulous companies have only God/Allah to fear, but that fear of God is far up there. Here in battleground Africa, it is the mercy of God that is protecting the people; God will have mercy on us.

We all know that people have to have medication when they are sick. The manufacturers know that none of the multiple, fragmented governments is evaluating the potency of these drugs, or even has the capability to evaluate the purity of any drug. Knowing these two facts, the pharmaceutical duplicating business has become very profitable; the only other industry that beats drug duplication is liquid gold.

With Africation, there is much to gain. This allows for the implementation of a controlling motherland watchdog with teeth to enforce its intent, while at the same time establishing standard for pharmaceuticals and the economic environment, to develop such institutions throughout the motherland.

13

OBVIOUS BENEFITS OF CONSOLIDATION/UNIFICATION

Consolidation allows for a greater pool of highly qualified and competent human resources in both sides of the arena. From the group that chooses to lead, there will be plenty of fine leaders to choose from; the best of the finest may lead. On the other hand, from the group that chooses to oppose, there will be plenty of like-minded individuals; and the best of the best may lead the opposition.

Concentration of her very scarce resource, which is now in the form of highly skilled labor, will encourage dramatic growth of frank industries within the entire African landscape. Growth here will be palpable, and it will differ very much from the traditional lackadaisical growth often promised by past enclave leaders.

Growth under Africation will be people and corporation driven as opposed to growth driven by government, which we all know is not sustainable. Besides, growth here will be in real time to be realized and utilized in a very short period, never to exceed two to three years, as opposed to growth in the past, usually calibrated in multiples of five, ten, and some inhuman time. Most of us will probably die before some of the promised growths of enclave governments are realized.

This time, growth will come in the form of industries such as:

(a) The electrical power sector. Engineers from all parts of this motherland will coalesce to form an electrical grid system that meets the need of the entire motherland. These engineers will transcend tribal national, language and cultural barriers. These engineers might speak different languages, but their professional language and engineering principles will be the same. Once a standard is agreed upon, it then becomes a template of care to be duplicated into every major sector of the motherland.

(b) Other isolated industries, such as the medical industry in this dear motherland, are industries in need of standardization of care as well as standardization of the medication used during treatment. Such industries will only crop up into existence under the protective arms of a unified motherland.

(c) Existing small companies will begin to transform into corporations. Africation brings with it a bigger market share as well as dramatic increases in revenue. From there, positive spillover effects will trickle down to the entire motherland.

The benefit of revamping the existing fragmented status quo is quite huge and very immediate. Whatever generation is able to implement such an overhaul should, with absolute certainty, be present to see and enjoy the benefits of the fruits of their labor (i.e., a much-developed motherland).

As of now, if the status quo continues, none of the living, be it a newly born baby or newly graduated high school scholars, will be in a position to see such development within the existing enclaves. Facing such grim odds, it is imperative that consolidation and rapid development be initiated at blitz speed.

Consolidation cannot be one of those very gradual and prolonged processes. This has already been tried by the OAU. That, we should all know by now, was a failure. The reasons for its failure are:

(i) It lacked the involvement of the people. The OAU never attempted to reach out to the people it represented. It only reached out to the leaders of a flawed system.

(ii) OAU lacked the will to draw a line in the sand and pronounce an expedited consolidation date within our lifetime.

In the face of such a show of incompetence, the OAU in this book is relegated to the position of a Boy Scout; where it paraded the boyish leaders of the current, flawed systems. The current Africans Union is the same as the OAU in that they both have the same flaws.

The greatest generation of the motherland is yet to be seen. That title will be reserved for whatever generation is able to implement the consolidation of this motherland. By the way, that title is still up for grabs. Those who need it will grab it. Our parents and grandparents had no need to grab for it, because all their needs were right there in their backyards. There, it was grown or was harvested naturally. Hopefully, this generation, generation alpha, will go for it and get all Africans involved in this great cause of Africation.

Africa likes to talk about how it has been looted of its wealth in the past. The fact is, Africa is still being looted of its wealth in the form of poor trade deals, because she comes to the bargaining table as a fragment and a weak bargainer. She does not present herself as a single wholesale buyer, but rather as a loan retailer buyer. Africation will convert Africa into a wholesale buyer overnight. She will approach the bargaining table with leverage. Anybody speaking for or representing 850 million people has leverage. Africans ought to start using this leverage. Hence, it is about time that we cut our losses, put our efforts together, get our act together, and start this African antelope leaping forward.

14

ELECTRICITY: A UNIVERSAL AFRICAN PATHOSIS

Few, if any, countries in Africa right now have the financial capacity to build mega electrical power structures such as hydroelectric plants. Given the current geopolitical situation in the global arena, I do not see any extra-African donors in line to sponsor or support the construction of such mega projects.

Projects of this type will require huge financial resources as well as an army of highly skilled labor.

Existing African enclaves do not have such funds or labor all by themselves. Based upon that formula, I can therefore predict with a great degree of certainty that the electrical problems of individual African states are here to stay as long as the fundamental issue of unification is not resolved. Simply put, the unification of Africa has a direct impact on the electricity-generating capacity of the entire continent.

Perhaps under unification, the potential, at least, does exist to coalesce the money and the scarce skilled labor that are needed to build and maintain such mega projects.

All the electrical problems plaguing most African countries have been viewed as national, or country based, problems. The reality is that these are not as localized as they are perceived. Instead, they are more generalized or regional problems at the very least. Blackouts are as synonymous with many African enclaves as they are with Africa as a whole. The standard joke during a power outage is "welcome to Africa this is our way of life". Since it is obvious that the problem is generalized, a better approach to solving such a common problem is with a holistic approach.

For those African enclaves buying into the notion that newly-found wealth, mainly liquid gold, will solve their electrical problems, I will urge their leaders and their citizens to take heed: that road has been traveled on before by others, and the problems still exist.

During my high school days, I had the perception that electrical power problems were a direct repercussion of corruption, because governmental officers pocketed part of the funds. Gradually, I came to understand the problem better, and I began to realize that corruption is a very small part of the big picture.

The various African governments by themselves are doing the best they can with the existing flawed system. To make matters worse, access, demand, and utilization of electricity have been rising exponentially.

Africation, with all its advantages and disadvantages, will put the African people and her leaders in a better position to tackle this problem as a single African problem, as opposed to the status quo of every enclave tackling this problem individually. Only through unification will the thoughts and dreams of constructing mega power structures become realistic a dream; otherwise, existing enclaves, given their size and wealth, cannot even dream of such an endeavor.

Aside from the occasional blackout here and there, failure to reach a comprehensive solution to this problem will mean a continued negative impact on to the continent. The palliative cure adapted by the African people is far worse than a regular power outage.

Individual African countries by themselves are big consumers of portable generators, or should I say backup generators. Collectively, the entire African continent is a super consumer of backup generators. To make matters worse, those millions of backup generators are bought at two to three times above global market prices. This is all money that Africa does not have in the first place. Such money could have been better spent elsewhere.

Africation is the antidote to this generalized African pathosis

15

THE AFRICAN BRAIN DRAIN

To propagate prosperity in the motherland, funds must be available. These funds are generally available in two forms:

(a) Direct inheritance.

(b) Blood, sweat, and tears in combination with a credit line.

Anybody who is an adult today knows how difficult it is to acquire credit from an institute or any given body throughout the entire motherland. With the exception of the 0.2% who have direct political leverage, this leaves 99.8% of the population unable to acquire short-term or long-term loans. Hence, a genuinely enterprising individual has virtually no chance at raising the minimum credit line. Few will get to realize that the existing system in their country or regional area does not allow the acquisition of credit or investment capital, irrespective of how hardworking one may be within his or her society. The result is that such individuals will end up migrating to other parts of their societies. Most of the time, migration is from the village to the ever-present, enlarged, 24-hour market centers that we all love to call cities. Criticism of the cities is not what the issue is about, but rather to navigate a path through which Africa can emerge out of this pattern of migration.

For the most part, the path of migration out of countries or enclaves starts in the village. My view of migration is always positive; if one's soul is not happy at home, then pick up and move. Home is where you make it to be, and besides, there is no need to stay home and be miserable; migration is sometimes refreshing to the soul.

In its current form, migration from the village is a very good sign. It shows that all those who have migrated or are migrating to the cities are the enterprising and the risk takers. They are not losers. They are potential winners in search of opportunities. They have taken a big risk into the unknown; they cannot, therefore, be classified as lazy, idle or useless. It is the system that has failed the migrants. Their migration have shown their willingness to take whatever is out there.

Upon their arrival out there, most will come to realize that these cities are inflicted with the same limited opportunities they left back in the village. Newly found employment opportunities are barely enough to maintain their survival on a daily basis. Nevertheless, throughout the entire continent, these determined migrants continue to hang on and do whatever penny-paying jobs he or she can get to ensure survival for the day.

As migration continues, a good chunk of the highly enterprising and now educated individuals take off for overseas. Like their brothers and sisters from the villages, this time it is from the cities and towns off to the Big Apple and the likes of it. Once again, they prove their determination and will to survive.

With unification, all fifty-three doors within Africa will be open to all African youths. Attending universities within the continent will become a viable option for the future brains of Africa, and corporations that emerge out of Africation will be attractive employment opportunities to all. Certainly, Africation will not bring about a complete halt to the African brain drain; after all, this has been going on for the past thirty to forty years. Africation will, however, cut down on the population lost to this phenomenon, perhaps from a couple of millions to a lesser number, such as half of the existing millions.

Though Africation seeks to assimilate and integrate the entire continent, there is that possibility of opening up the floodgates to the few thriving enclaves. With the fear of being overrun by less fortunate Africans, speed bumps should be adapted temporarily to curb and control such possible scenarios. Another possible alternative is to have a five year freeze on inter-African immigration, with an exception given to all legitimate commercial immigration. However, these are barely suggestions; I am sure that better remedies would be worked out.

The ultimate goal is Africation. Difficulties will be encountered along the way, but at least these will be difficulties in the right direction as opposed to difficulties within the flawed system as it is today.

Africation, therefore, is a practical plug to the African brain drain. Failure to plug this drain will result in the continuation of the status quo.

16

REGIONAL ECONOMIES SAME AS STATUS QUO – JUST ANOTHER DELAYING TACTIC

This is a positive move to begin with. It gives the perception of taking huge, positive steps forward into consolidation, but why prolong the pain any further? Besides, this arrangement does not address the problem of the physical links between cities or countries, such as:

(a) It does not call for transportation routes, such as inter-enclave roads, interstate roads, inter-country roads, or railways, to be built immediately.

(b) It does not eliminate the need for customs officers and guarantee their total absence from any inter-enclave border crossing within those regional economic zones.

(c) It does not have a short timeline for consolidating any of the economic financial structures, such as banks and ministries, into one voice to speak for all.

Therefore, upon this above note (or lack thereof), it is wise to conclude that these arrangements of regional economic zones are simply delaying tactics, the usual huffing and puffing and no motion. It is obvious that the intention is good, but the fundamental structure of these arrangements is flawed. These regional economic zones and unions are likely to fail, unless the problems above are addressed favorably, because the built in flaw in the African design is still present.

When all is said and done, it will take only one regional economic member to collapse the entire regional alliance. As we all know, far too often, a new government takes control by the cheapest and easiest method via a coup d'état. Under this situation, every agreement and arrangement goes back to square one; who, then, becomes the enforcer of the previous treaty or regional economic alliance? Sanctions within the region will be counterproductive, because one would have to deal with the problem of aggravating the situation and increasing the potency of the black market.

There is also the interest of the individual heads of state for their own people. If there is any degree of implication that one side loses more than it gains from an alliance, this argument would be used by the coup d'état leader to stir up emotions and cause the alliance to lose its popularity. Loopholes will begin to creep up. What, then, should be done here? Sanctions will not do; one can't punish the suffering, because they are likely to argue that they have seen worse. Hence, the phrase "can't beat a dead horse" will come into mind.

Thus, this idea of regionalized economics is simply a waste of time. It is just a drop of water in the bucket to quench the thirst of Africans. It will not work as it is proposed. Regionalization will find itself in the same hall of failure as the OAU, though some will argue it is already there.

The underlying problem has not been tackled, the complete overhaul of the entire regional economics, and therefore of the entire continent, linking not only economies, but physical land masses as well as political entities into a unified motherland with a single agenda to pursue. This, of course, will only be realized by Africation.

This drip, drip, drip, theory has been practiced before by our parents' generation and its leaders. The result is minute gains that cannot be quantified within any meaningful time. As a result, frustration develops among the people, civil unrest erupts, anarchy sets in, sending entire societies back to square one; at times, to a worse predicament than where we started during the immediate post independence. That is the legacy of our parents' failed generation.

Those who do not learn from the mistakes of their parents will not remember those mistakes, and surely they will repeat them. As a reminder, the OAU, as we all know, was a disaster.

The current AU is a bandage to the disasters of the OAU because of the failure of this body to address a comprehensive unification within a given and palpable time frame that all Africans can relate to, live through, and experience.

This AU has not made any genuine effort to reach out to the African people, nor has it facilitated the formation of grass root movements but instead it continues on the path of the belated OAU by focusing on the heads of states.

This AU is built upon a very faulty and flawed foundation. Though the intentions are good and great, the design flaw within the current African system is not addressed with the degree of urgency or priority that such a problem deserves.

Yes, this AU is already outperforming its predecessors, the OAU. This AU definitely does not want to see a repeat of Rwanda; with the ghost of Rwanda still haunting the entire continent, the AU is forced to position itself to intervene in future Rwanda like scenario. This is about the most that will come out of the AU, therefore; the presence of this organization as of yet, is to serves as another delaying tactic put in place to buy another twenty five or fifty years of the African fragmented status quo.

This generation must not follow into the footsteps of its parents. It's obvious that they have failed, due in part to their preoccupation with the many delaying tactics they encountered in their attempt to achieve African unification. This generation will have to stay focused and keep their eyes on the ball. Africation is the ball, and the goal is African unification as soon as possible.

17

AFRICA'S SEAT AT THE UNITED NATIONS

This body is a global entity that must be reckoned with. This body has been established as the global finger that rocks and shapes the paths of most nations.

Africa today has no significant role in the UN. Africa's role is more of an observer than a mover or a shaker. If this trend or status quo continues, all fifty-three enclaves of Africa will continue to play the same role they have been assigned to play, which is based on an agreed upon schedule.

Africation will seek to halt this trend, to rotate and redirect it into a path that fairly represents and suits Africa's interest, as well as the interest of other global nations.

All fifty-three sister enclaves within Africa, as the status quo is today, can only attempt to set the agenda, at most, and surely they cannot influence the outcome. Besides, the collective interest of Africa is never satisfied; only the selfish interest of the individual enclave is satisfied.

Knowing that as an absolute fact, it is therefore in the interest of Africa to have one voice and only one voice speaking for the motherland at the table of the UN. Then, eventually, this voice must start to seek a permanent status at the table with all the bells and whistles that come along with it, including its fair share of financial responsibility. Meeting its financial responsibility is very important, because failure to do so will leave the perception that Africa is taking on free meals.

Under the status quo of rotating nations, the collective interest of Africa will never get an opportunity to be represented at the table of the UN. To illustrate the poor and marginal representation that Africa has been dealt, I will have to take you back to the pre-Second Gulf War days. At that time, Guinea was on stage, representing the interest of Africa on the usual rotation of nations at the UN. The perception, therefore, was that Guinea represented the interest of Africa. The actual reality on the ground is that Guinea represented only the interest of Guinea. Guinea knew that, and across the oceans, every nation knew that as well, but the collective continental Africa either did not know or did not care. If she did not care, the goal here is to make her care, because in the global arena, there are consequences for a nation's action or inaction.

Every nation across the ocean knows for sure that it was much cheaper and easier to satisfy and influence Guinea, rather than it would have been to woo the entire African continent.

The obvious move from the developed world, then, was to meet with Guinea directly, give Guinea what Guinea wants, and then it has, very cheaply, the support of Guinea and therefore the support of Africa. Though this is a perception, the reality is that perception is 50% of the game of life.

During the pre-Second Gulf War days, it was perceived that Guinea was representing Africa, but on the other hand, she was not given the appropriate respect she deserved while she carried out her assigned role at the UN. This was clearly obvious and publicly stated by highly respected minds, such as Henry Kissinger, whose statement on national TV was to dismiss the role of countries like Guinea, as being a very poor country with a small population that is far removed from the issue being discussed and who all of a sudden gets a visit from the French and American leaders, which is very demeaning.

Others on TV, with reference to Angola, denounced its importance by saying some of the most geopolitically insignificant nations in the world are basking in the role of importance. With such views, and the public marginalization of Africa's representatives at the UN, it should be quite obvious that the current system does nothing but injustice to Africa as a whole.

The obvious antidote to such blatant marginalization is Africation. Under Africation, the representative at the UN will definitely represent the interest of Africa; he or she will be one voice that speaks for the entire motherland.

With one voice representing the interest of Africa, given its size, it would be only a matter of time before its permanent status at the table of the UN is achieved.

Skeptics will say, "Why does India, given its population, not get a permanent status at the UN?" The obvious answer here is two fold.

(a) India, despite its billion people, has a very small footprint on this earth's real estate. Africa, on the other hand, has a much larger footprint; this could be leverage, if used wisely.

(b) India's permanent seat at the UN will have to happen. As of now, she has not set her mind on that seat yet. She fully understands the value of going to the bargaining table with leverage. That is what she is currently working on.

Africa sits on a huge piece of real estate. It must realize what it is sitting on; to put very simply, it is one of the seven continents of this world. Hence, if Africa, an entire continent, cannot secure a permanent place at the table of the UN, then the UN must cease to call itself the United Nations. Perhaps it must be renamed by one-seventh of this world (i.e., Africa) as the "un-United Nations;" in this way, it still gets to maintain its abbreviation.

However, failure to secure a permanent seat at the table in the short runs right after unification is understandable. Therefore, the motherland must never walk away from the UN. Her participation at all times is very crucial; however, this participation should be lukewarm. This is because the reality in this modern time is that a back chair in the room where the decisions are made is much better than a chair out of that room, because out of that room, all information is secondhand. At that point, the perception of others is what would be handed down.

Once again, the mistakes of our grandparents should not be repeated in this modern era. Africation is the only way out of the marginalized role to which the individual African states, as well as the collective African continent, have been relegated to for all these years. Perhaps such a marginalized role is acceptable to our parents, but it is definitely not acceptable to our generation. Failure of this generation to aggressively reach out for the ultimate African destiny will put this generation in the same lackadaisical and passive boat as our parents. Yes, they were part of the generation that missed the African unification boat the first time around. Back in those days, the wisdom of Nkrumah was not fully appreciated. Besides, at that time, all those newly independent African states had delusions of grandeur; today, all of Africa is aware that such delusions did not materialize. Africation, therefore, is a practical and realistic dream within reach of all African nations.

AFRICATION LEADS TO AFRICAN PATRIOTISM

Patriotism in modern day Africa is at its lowest. African patriotism will become a phenomenon for every African when we arrive at unification. At that point, it will not matter what one's racial orientation is; whether it is Arab, Caucasian, Indian, or Black African, the bottom line is that African will be the nationality. That will be a patriotic phrase that is simple and straight to the point, hence the unnecessary need for further explanation, such as X-Y-Z lies next to Ghana, or is that West, East, South, etc.

On the flipside, today we are Africans. We have African physical features, we have African accents, and we have many other attributes associated with Africans. The people of Africa, however, do not carry an African passport, nor do they have a single African voice that represents African interest in the global arena. Instead, we have many little voices that attempt to represent the interest of Africa.

These many little voices often represent the interests of the individual enclaves, whose interests are usually in direct relation to the interest of donor nations. This is "drive-through imperialism." In case you miss the point, drive-through imperialism describes the practice of donor nations whenever they find themselves in a situation where they need international approval for their policies. Representative of such donor nations will literally drive or fly through the African continent, buying up support for their cause as they go. Drive-through imperialism will forever prevent the interest of the African people from coinciding with the interest of the African governments. Africation will bring about a coincidence of all African interest.

We are all familiar with the phrase from Julius Gaius Caesar who said "divide and conquer." Well, this has long been the case in Africa; there are multiple African identities instead of a unified African identity. A unified African identity paves the way to patriotism. Africation, therefore, is a path to African patriotism.

We would all expect African leaders to be the most patriotic of all Africans; however, a closer look at the behavior patterns of these leaders has left many wondering why an increasing number of these leaders have been opting to retire in the lands of extra-African countries. The obvious follow-up question to this is why don't they go to one of the other fifty three African countries? Surely any one of the fifty-three will gladly accommodate these ex-leaders, granting them all the bells and whistles that come along with their status.

Another pressing issue of concern is why African leaders often save their hard-earned millions in the banks of extra-African countries. When will these leaders get the obvious point? Money saved in those banks will always be subjected to being frozen. Worst of all, this money could have been saved in African-based banks, where it could be better used to support domestic African institutions; after all, African-based banks have, over time, proved themselves to be quite reliable, perhaps even more reliable than most African governments.

Though it is fair to question the patriotism of African leaders, on the final analysis, they are indeed patriots who are swimming upstream against the current of the flawed African design.

19

IDEOLOGICAL DEFICIT

Vision moves a community forward. A society that lacks vision will find itself as a spinning wheel, because it lacks the concentration of momentum and drive to bring it over the hump, thereby keeping the ball rolling.

Yes, it is true that today, in Africa, many leaders have their own visions of where and how they will take their nations over the hump. This, at the end of the day, will be a monumental task, because African people are being lead in multiple directions by multiple visionaries (i.e., their leaders). The net gain is stagnation and commotion, but not movement or motion.

On the other hand, a consolidated motherland will have a single visionary being advised by multiple visionaries, but ultimately, only the visions of the consolidated leader will be acted upon. This allows for the people of the motherland to focus on a sole path toward a vision, instead of the multiple visions and multiple paths we have been on for the last fifty years. With a concentration of the people's collective effort, be it intellectual, physical skills, or resources, a collective forward leap will become a reality within a very short and realistic timeframe.

With a unified vision, the collective "African antelope" will leap into life on its own, totally independent of any single leader. Africa and its people will find themselves with a vision and a unified policy. With a consolidated policy in place, the dealings of Africa with other nations will become transparent, consistent, and globally comprehended.

If Africa looks around, all other major nations have clear, distinctive, well-published policies on every day-to-day issue. Their policies are transparent. Transparency saves time; a lack of transparency would have resulted in a large amount of time being spent on tailoring policies for every trading partner or transaction. Most of all, transparency shows the rules, the guidelines, and the path that has to be taken to achieve x-y-zee. Very simply, with consolidation, the status quo ideological deficit will be transformed into ideological vision. Such an ideological vision is what Africation will bring into reality.

20

DINOSAUR GENERATIONS OF AFRICA

Our great-grandparents, grandparents, most of our parents, and some of us today were raised and lived a life stuck in the ways of the dinosaurs. We all know what happened to the dinosaurs; they became extinct.

The motherland is much too versatile a survivor for extinction, but it will be further marginalized into the position of a vestigial land.

The interest of Africa would be best secured by Africans interested in the future of Africa. In this world, today and in the future, battles are chosen and fought to coincide with the interest of nations.

Africans, we must wake up! My brothers and sisters, wake up! Stop pretending to be asleep, stop ignoring the facts on the ground. They will not resolve themselves, nor will they go away. The facts on the ground have to be dealt with. Africa's interest will only be secured from within, not from outside. Remember Rwanda, where a half million, people were killed while all of Africa kept on pretending it was asleep, or that the problem would resolve itself, hopefully by these scenarios:

(1) When the Rwandans get tired;

(2) When the Rwandans run out of people to kill (they almost did);

(3) By divine intervention.

Meanwhile, the massacre went on for a good while. To all Africans, now is the time to start speaking out, not only in your homes or among friends. You must speak out in the streets alongside strangers, you must speak out in masses, and you must speak out peacefully and conspicuously.

Peaceful public protests are never spontaneous; they have to be organized and coordinated. Reasonable men and women will have to start having interest in the welfare of the motherland, we will have to be ready to put our boots on the ground and march towards the ultimate African destiny. . Once again, it is not healthy, at this stage of the continent's development, to have a mass of brothers and sisters stand by and watch the world roll by. Those who did that were the dinosaur generation; our parents did just that. It is, therefore, up to all enlightened brothers and sisters to set the movement of consolidation into motion. Eventually, the siblings of these enlightened Africans will come to respect the collective effort of those who made a stand when history is reviewed.

Much of African history in today's global culture is pretty bleak. Not much is mentioned in global history or textbooks. The number of pages allocated to the text regarding Africa's history is regressing; fewer reports on major events have been reported. A few more pages are allocated to farming, wars, and today's AIDS epidemic. Our parents and grandparents complained about the omission or marginalization of Africa's history in global history books. Stop right here! My brothers and sisters, wake up from your sleep. History is being made. Participate, go out in the streets, stand among strangers, gather in masses, and peacefully voice your opinions. Those who fail to complain and participate have accepted the status quo. This generation of today is enlightened. It must break away from the ways of its dinosaur ancestors; it must not stand by and watch like the true dinosaurs did.

21

FREEDOM IN AFRICA IS RELATIVE: FREEDOM PROPER AFRICA MUST STRIVE FOR

Today Africa enjoys relative freedom. Some of us have seen better than relative freedom. Freedom proper is what we ought to have, and that is what the motherland seeks.

The perception that all enclaves in Africa today have independence and freedom in this 21st century is a fallacy. Africa and the people of Africa are not free. We have been held in virtual bondage since the division of Africa started, way back in time.

This virtual bondage today is in the form of miniature, multiple enclaves called countries; their borders serve to contain all African citizens within these demarcated boundaries. For those skeptics who believe that they have freedom simply because they can hop around from one demarcated area to the other (country-to-country), that is simply an illusion; those skeptics must ask themselves if they have the same access and opportunities out of their demarcated zone. Of course, the answer would be in the negative. That being the case, these skeptics ought to consider joining the crowd.

No business in operation today has operating freedom and access that is the same to all enclaves within the motherland. Therefore, freedom proper in today's Africa, my brothers and sisters, is just a fallacy.

Right at the borders of these demarcated zones are speed bumps in the form of various government authorities of each individual nation. These speed bumps serve to slow down progress, and they are also repressive obstacles to the African people. Enforcement of these repressive policies is implemented by:

(a) The presence of a customs department to tax and regulate commercial activities across demarcated zones, thereby keeping commercial activity within the proverbial box or country.

(b) Army or military border patrols have the same repressive effect on Africans, thereby keeping them within their proverbial box or country.

(c) Multiple countries, multiple governments with no strings attached among themselves or between each other, are just clusters of islands side by side. To make matters worse, these clusters of islands are all individual nations on this great motherland with their own isolated agendas.

Yes, the presence of your own government with any of the above three policies has qualified you as a free range African, free to run around, do business, or practice politics as long as you stay within the country's borders (i.e., the range).

The people of Africa today have to face the fact that, Africans only have the perception of freedom as free countries. Freedom proper, which Africans should enjoy as the sons and daughters of the motherland, is yet to be seen. This freedom is a right that today's Africans must seek until the house of Africa tears down all its inherited containment walls, allows free movement, and allows unscheduled and unsupervised transactions and exchanges between brothers and sisters of the same motherland. Only then will freedom proper, be achieved.

In conclusion, I propose relocating the border guards and the customs officers to the greater peripheral borders of the motherland, now there is the natural rest position for the guard, as well as the ultimate goal of Africation.

22

MONO-INDUSTRIES (ONE PRODUCT WONDER COUNTRIES)

The greatest perception of most African nations as mono-industries is just as the phrase implies: one nation, one product. We all know of:

Gambia for peanuts;

Mauritania for iron ore;

Zambia for copper;

Libya for oil, etc.

If this trend continues in the next ten years, then why would it not continue to be the case in the next twenty or thirty years, or should I say forever?

On the flipside, a stride to marginalize the effects of mono-industries will only come into realization under consolidation. Any reasonably-minded individual should know that every industry has its ups and downs. Just as there are good harvests and bad harvests, it is normal in the cycle of nature to have periods of glut and those periods that falls below expectations.

Those periods that fall below expectations have been devastating to the economies of mono-industrial nations, to their health, and to the psyche of the entire motherland. In order for motherland Africa to be self reliant, she ought to have diversified economic enclaves with multiple sources and access to all the resources within the continent; as the status quo is right now, multiple sources and access to all of Africa's resources are available at the full disposal of non-African nations. These nations have always used motherland Africa as a discount store for raw materials, which are priced dead cheap because a mono-industrial nation sells its only product to its only buyer who is always an extra-African nation. This is not because these external buyers offer the best price (we all know that this is not the case), but simply because these mono-industrial nations have no choice but to sell to external buyers. These external buyers then turn around, repackage, and brand these products, and resell them to other nations within the motherland. What a ride poor Africa is being taken through. She is treated with very little respect simply because she begs for it, yearns for it, and has tolerated it all these years with no move to change her situation.

Hence, it is up to the very few reasonably-minded and educated sons and daughters of this motherland to seriously reform the situation. We must change the status quo and mobilize progressive, like-minded brothers and sisters in a unified march forward to the consolidation of this motherland. Only then can we offer those mono-industrial enclaves more choices of buyers.

This time, buyers can make the transformation without the speed bumps. Eventually, perhaps, excess production will be sold out to the external market at reasonable and fair market prices.

Our current governments are inadequate in their capacity to bring unification to this continent. They have the intent, but they lack the vision and the will to effectuate the movement forward into consolidation. It is the people, in this case, the reasonably-minded people who have the power to bring this vision into motion.

A very simple fact that has to be realized is that non-enlightened brothers and sisters, do not and might never understand the benefit of consolidation because, as far as they are concerned, there are no benefits or changes in their lives but rather a continuation of the status quo, that was the long held view of the dinosaur generation. Realizing these facts on the ground, it is therefore reasonable in the short term, at least, to discount these brothers and sisters until unification is achieved. Then, we can continue on the track of integrating all unreasonable brothers and sisters into the cause of moving the motherland forward.

On the contrary, if this motherland and all its enclaves choose to wait until all of its people are fully ready for integration, or when all the regional economies are matured, it is safe to say this will happen when the citizens of all enclaves and states have become reasonable and educated. This is a very unlikely scenario that is not likely to happen in the next ten, twenty, or one hundred years or more.

Knowing these facts, the burden of consolidation lies on the shoulders of all reasonably-minded brothers and sisters. After all, decisions made today that usually gravely impact the lives of our non-enlightened brothers and sisters are made by the very few under the banner of governmental institutions and policies. Reasonably-minded brothers and sisters have to realize that the power to change the course of the future is in their hands, not fifty years from now or five years into the future, but today, tomorrow or within these days, Africation is within reach. Like-minded citizens have the numbers to become activists, the numbers to voice their desires, and the ability to parade peacefully on a routine basis, unrelenting, continuously working until unification is achieved.

The movement of unification must crop up within every enclave, and then it will coalesce to bridge the gap between nations. Where do you stand, my reasonably-minded brothers and sisters? Are you a recruit or a recruiter? You have no choice. This is your motherland, not the land of your government or tribe; this is it. Africans have to pick a side. There are no more free meals in life.

At this stage of the game, Africa cannot afford to have its reasonable citizens stand by while its fate is being decided by external nations from across the oceans. For those people who love to play it safe, believing that their opinion or stance does not matter, hell no—it does matter; every single mind is a mind of value. Every single body is a child of this motherland. This is our land, these are our resources; we should decide when to sell according to the simple laws of supply and demand, not to the laws of desperation as the status quo is today. This desperate undervalued selling of her resource is what Africation will seek to halt and alter. Thereby positioning these mono-industrial nations to sell at fair market price.

THE DEBT BURDEN

The debt burden in Africa is crippling, to put it mildly, but it is ironic that everyone is trying to do something about Africa's crippling debt burden except for Africa herself. From sporadic peaceful protests in the west during G8 summit meetings to organized protests in Washington during the annual World Bank and IMF meetings, and from rock musicians like Bono and Bruce Springsteen to actor Brad Pitt, all have good intentions, and I must add that all of these uncoordinated efforts are now bearing fruit. But where are the Africans? What are they doing? I do not see any African organization out there peacefully demonstrating for an improvement in the quality of life for all Africans. Hopefully, this is what Africation will be all about.

The recent G8 summit in Scotland specifically focused on the question of debt relief for the world's poorest countries, and whenever the poorest of the poor were mentioned, Africa was no exception, and this breaks my heart. But let me stop whining, and let's look at the proposal on the table for which the United Kingdom is the chief proponent through its Chancellor of the Exchequer, Gordon Brown. Under this plan, countries that qualify will get a 100% write-off of all monies owed to all international lending institutions. This should give them a clean slate to start off with.

Then, on top of that, the G8 will pledge a certain amount each year in aid to these nations. Since this is a fixed commitment, these nations will be allowed to borrow against the pledged amounts. There are conditions to it, which is why not every country in the motherland with debt relief needs will qualify.

The fine print for pre-qualification is good governance, the rule of law, and a path to a market economy. The intent here is good and honorable; all those involved in this effort should be applauded, but to me, this is like filing for bankruptcy. The answer to Africa's economic debt burden is not to write off its debts. Writing off the debt is just one of many steps that should be taken to arrive at sustainable economic growth. We must remember that the choice of indebtedness was not imposed upon us; it was voluntary, thanks by the failed generation. Inaction by our parents to rapidly consolidate the African continent has left the entire continent weak and unable to develop its economy. We made that choice, and I think it is ludicrous for present administrations to place the blame on previous regimes; if you assume power over a nation, you assume its problems, too. The big difference between these present leaders and the previous leaders is that the present leaders are in a position to bring about rapid Africation if they choose to do so.

There are many reasons for the debt situation that we now face in the motherland: corruption, misplaced priorities, political instability, and insecurity, which forces governments to use limited resources in their reckless purchase of arms. Fear of these reasons is why the G8 is using the same criteria for pre-qualification in the write-off scheme. It is my belief, though, that the greater reason for the debt predicament in Africa is due in part to the unnatural design flaw still present in the African system. (i.e. fragmentation)

Africa must stop acting as if it is the duty of richer nations to do something about our economic plight. It is our duty to get past the colonialism and low expectation syndrome, and begin to work toward lifting ourselves out of poverty to sustainable economic growth. This is not to say that we do not welcome a helping hand from friendly nations; we certainly do welcome help, and heaven knows we need it, but it should not be the answer. After all, we were not the only ones under the shackles of foreign domination; some of the world's newly emerging markets, namely India as a case in point, were under the same domination as we were—but they have come to realize that the world does not owe them a living. Thus, today, they have a growing economy that is a potential threat to the world's largest economic powers.

I have never seen anyone get rich through a welfare system. Welfare does help to keep one in existence while one is in transition, but many people in a welfare system never make it out of transition. They even die while in transition; that is surely a tragedy. Such is the transition legacy of O.A.U and now A.U, Hopefully, Africation will not take a lifetime to achieve.

If we have debts written off for the motherland without the political will and resolve to transform our motherland into a place of growth and prosperity for all, African nations will spiral right back into the situation from where we had started. Even worse, in such a scenario, the write-off scheme could become another big welfare scheme; the efforts of all those well-meaning, well-intentioned people would have been wasted.

As a reminder, that road has been traveled before. Our grandparents, in the immediate post-colonial era, started with no debt, and in most cases, they started with healthy reserves; it's obvious they failed us miserably, then why should the present generation expect to do better, especially with more obstacles on the ground today than there were back in the 1960s?

My brothers and sisters, we need to act now. This transformation needs to be realized in our lifetime, and God knows this is not only possible but necessary.

We cannot continue to have ourselves being bailed out all the time; we need to face up to the challenges ourselves.

In my early studies of the reason why people submit to governments or organized societies, I learned that the firstly we need governments to maintain law and order. Secondly, to acquire the "good life," meaning the right to have a fair chance of economic prosperity. When any of these is not forthcoming, there will always certainly be anarchy, and this has been the problem with most of the motherland.

In the motherland, there is a tendency for us to depend on the manna-from-the-sky syndrome before we act. That is why we have been in the state we are in for such a long period of time.

Every single individual born to a low income family has at least three major opportunities to break out of their predicament, to rise to the top of their social ladder.

The first opportunity is through education. One born to a low income family takes his or her education seriously; if one makes it through college, one has a 90% chance of making it to the upper middle class or higher.

The second opportunity for one born in a low income family is that if he or she has some high school or college education, and perhaps some naturally endowed talents, help, and good fortune, one is likely to catch a break, provided that one is good and is serious about developing that talent.

Third, one can enter the work force with some high school education, get some skills, and specialize; that will position anyone with a 60% chance of making it.

We can blame slavery, colonialism, nepotism, corruption, inept leadership, and all the isms there are to blame. We know there is plenty of blame to go around, but at the end of the day, unless WE THE PEOPLE RISE UP, we can never take our place in the world's economic community. Africation is a realistic and attainable possibility, so it's time to roll up our African sleeves and start leaping to our ultimate destiny, hopefully not to another of those very long development plans that we will never realize in our lifetimes.

SACRIFICES

24

RELOCATION OF BORDER GUARDS AND CUSTOM OFFICERS BETWEEN COUNTRIES TO THE PERIPHERAL OF THE MOTHERLAND

To move from the theoretical aspect of unification into the practical aspect of unification, the border guards and custom guards must be relocated. The following two reasons show the argument for the need for such relocation.

Suppressants to enterprises and dreamers:

1) TAX – the tax levied on enterprising individuals and businesses is grossly unfair to African businesses, both individual and corporate. Customs taxes are extremely restrictive; these taxes are highly effective in keeping all the commercial activities of any ambitious business entrepreneur or enterprise within the borders of the nation in which they do business. The intent of the government to have customs border officers is good at first glance, that is, to generate revenue for the government. But on further scrutiny, it has a regressive and restrictive effect that is much greater than the benefits it generates in revenue. Assuming the customs border officers are extremely honest, with a zero tolerance for corruption, an entrepreneur based on the coast has to go through four to six different customs stops to move his or her merchandise to the interior of the motherland, where demand for the products is great (refer to diagram R2). The thought of multiple customs

stops and change points, which delay commercial transactions, is discouraging. This discouraging thought by itself leads to the suppression of any entrepreneur's dreams. Suppressed entrepreneurs have their activities limited and restricted within the borders of a single nation, where they can stay out of reach of the customs border officers. In turn, this restriction leads to the regression of all ambitious entrepreneurs, thereby preventing African firms from acquiring the corporate status and size to compete effectively, both domestically and globally. In short, ambitious entrepreneurs within any of today's African countries have their thoughts and dreams caged, so movement is only within their borders.

On the other hand, there are truly determined entrepreneurs who are determined to test the current system (status quo). These are the most enterprising of the entrepreneurs, or the toughest of the tough, who have ventured out of their restrictive borders to conduct businesses in other sister nations. These entrepreneurs will quickly find their profit margins being vaporized due to:

(a) Delays and more delays at each demarcated border (customs border); and

(b) The rising costs of production and the rising costs of doing business due to multiple customs duties and tax expenses incurred on the way to the final business destination.

Sooner or later, these entrepreneurs and enterprises will not be able to sustain the presence of rising costs. They will eventually be forced to cut down or scale down their activities from regional or continental intentions to simply local and domestic activities, where they are surely out of the reach of the customs border officers. Yes, again, these are restrictive and regressive tax at their best.

The figure below shows a boatload of motorbikes from extra-African nations; it also shows how these bikes are disseminated throughout the coastal enclaves.

R1= -at port of entry, a shipload of motorbike unloads
-ship pays tax at port of entry
-ship pays tax one time only

R2= -motorbikes loaded onto a truck at port of entry
-truck pays tax as it leaves initial port of entry
-truck pays tax as it enters another enclave
-for every enclave, truck pays tax two times
-paying tax two times is a conservative estimate; this could easily be three times, four times, and up.

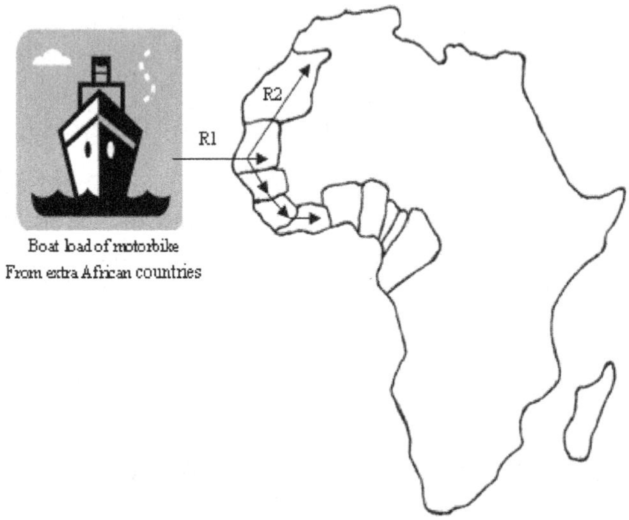

2) There are fewer taxes and fewer hurdles for foreign corporations. From outside Africa—Asia, Europe, etc.—corporate firms already have the strength and money to

conduct business globally. But when these corporations arrive at the doors of an African nation, they have to pay tax only once (refer to the above diagram, as shown in R1). That is, at the main port of entry where their merchandise is being delivered, from then on, it's free-wheeling; there are no more taxes, and it's profit all the way to the bank. For those skeptics, it's obvious that the African entrepreneur has less money, less access, four times more physical restriction, and four times the rising cost of conducting the same or similar businesses in his or her own homeland than it is for his or her extra-African counterparts. Under such conditions, it is obvious to any ambitious African entrepreneur that the system is restrictive, regressive, and self defeating. The American phrase describes the situation best: "the decks are fully stacked against" all African businesses from the start. This one reason, all by itself, makes the argument why Africation is a must, it is an absolute necessity for the commercial development and general welfare of Africa..

25

CONTRIBUTION OF RICH AND BIG COUNTRIES VS. SMALL AND POOR

For starters, no country in Africa, from the global point of view, is rich. The entire continent is made up of poor counties, but among poor folks, wealth is relative. The small and poor countries do not have much to offer, but on the other hand, they have the least baggage.

By baggage, I mean that they have less social pathology, e.g., criminality by volume, tribal conflict, etc. The bottom line is whatever negative qualities they possess in the greater scheme of Africation, those pathologies will be insignificant. Besides, these small and poor countries present themselves as opportunities for investment and growth. They are, for the most part, huge virgin markets, so their net contribution mostly evens out and is positive toward the interest of the bigger and richer countries.

The bigger and richer countries have a lot to offer, perhaps too many of 'their negatives' to offer. The most positive potential contribution from these enclaves is the critical mass of educated elites and professionals they bring to the table from Day One. On the other hand, these big and rich enclaves carry a lot of baggage. They carry huge systemic and social pathologies.

Though these big and rich countries are potential markets, the reality, in the short run is, it would be much easier for companies from the big and rich enclaves to establish themselves in the small and poor enclaves than vice versa. Hence, the net contribution of the big and rich countries to union is more of a negative toward the interest of the small and poor enclaves. But this should not be a deterrent, if it is, then a motivating incentive is to think of the status quo and the price every individual enclave has been paying for any imported big ticket items. Sometimes, the price is two to three times greater than the actual global price. That is the price of independence as opposed to interdependence as a unified motherland.

The bottom line is that every country loses, but gains more right away. The good old American proverb says you've got to lose some to win some.

The countries of Africa have to understand and accept such words of wisdom. The sons and daughters of Africa must sacrifice their national identities and put up with the good, the bad, and the ugly for the greater good of motherland Africa.

Existing national borders have only been in place for the past fifty year, for those who would like to include colonial days then in that case; for one century only. Prior to colonial days great African nations and their leaders had to give up their centuries old national sovereignty for the existing flawed system of 53 nations. Though at that time, it was under pressure applied at the barrel of the gun, this time around it is under pressure of continuous marginalization and economic impoverishment.

The recent argument against the call to sacrifice national sovereignty is not as tall an order as president Mosisili will like his fellow Africans to believe. Thus, existing sovereignties will be replaced by a much bigger, versatile and viable entity, perhaps in the order of a United Nations of Africa.(UNA).

26

LEARNING INSTITUTIONS

Although these institutions exist today, they lack the prestige and mystique associated with top notch institutions. Therefore, a coalition of resources is necessary to modify some of the existing universities, to improve their practical functional purpose as well as their aesthetic appeal. These institutions will be reserved for the best and the brightest. These will be the fertile breeding grounds for the most aspiring sons and daughters in the motherland.

Prestigious universities should be put in place for every major field of higher education. These should be put in place simultaneously with the inception of a unified motherland. These institutions will set the standards for all professions, from engineering to medicine to the Judiciary.

In the process of establishing a higher education system for the sons and daughters of the motherland, one practical reality has to be taken into consideration.

Education for all, at inception, would be impossible. This would be a humungous task. Any attempt to fully integrate every pocket of illiteracy within the continent will lead to overextension and dispersal of limited resources. The net result of such a dispersion of educational resources is a deficiency at the highest level of education, which we all know is the most crucial need of the motherland. Therefore, we must begin by spending the most resources on higher levels of education. These universities should be fully equipped, with the best teachers and professors from all around the continent put together in a few universities to form Africa's version of an Ivy League. Along with the equipment and professors should come an appropriate infrastructure to make such an institution prestigious. For those skeptics, or utopians who believe all citizens should be educated from the get-go, they need to consider these three reasons.

(1) The cost of educating all. This would be astronomic in cash and kind; besides, both cash and kind are in limited supply.

(2) The time factor. Educating the masses will take a great deal of time, perhaps twenty to thirty years planning will be needed, unless the intention is to promise the people snake oil. Therefore, the motherland is much better off modifying the few existing institutions to meet its needs.

(3) The concentration of resources and effort leads to a potentiation of results. A critical mass of professionals will be attained within a very short time, within the lifetime of all those who sacrifice for motherland Africa. With an abundant supply of engineers and inexpensive steel, this will be a recipe for growth, development, employment, and most of all, it will be an opportunity to absorb those newly graduated professionals, right here within the motherland.

Thus, the need is great for a few selected Ivy League universities, perhaps ten to twenty such institutions that can hold Africa's own in the global arena. At the same time, other major higher learning institutions would be modified to meet the needs of a unified African people.

27

SELECTING A LEADER FOR THE MOTHERLAND

As the status quo is with regard to the heads of states, they should be left in their current positions for five years with immunity, not as heads of states, but as governors. At the end of those five years, should those governors wish to stay in the political arena, then they will have to change job positions. This time around, they have to seek a higher or lower political position within the motherland.

This reshuffling of talent would ensure the infusion of new ideas into the Union. At the same time, these out-going leaders (governors) would be free and available to advise the successive generation of leaders.

In regard to the selection of the overall leader for the motherland, these prerequisites ought to be strongly followed; any diversion from these should not be tolerated. These should be the basic prerequisites:

(a) A college education. This is an absolute must. A bachelor's degree, at the least, must be earned before one is qualified; societies and economies today have become very complex. The need for a leader who understands economic principles and their long term ramifications is a must. The days of the wise, natural-born leaders without formal educations are long gone. Such leaders will not pass muster in today's economies and politically correct societies. When enemies fight today, it is in the board room; their weapon of choice is economic strength. Brute strength alone will cost you the battle. The old-time notion that leaders need not be educated is a thing of the past. The motherland society intends to take a look into the future, not into the past.

(b) An age minimum. Wisdom, pure wisdom, is desirable. All great African village stories often associate wisdom with age. Yes, it is quite possible to have wisdom at a younger or youthful age, but the wisdom associated with youth is untested wisdom. Matured or aged wisdom has been tested; therefore, leaders of this great motherland must have matured wisdom. Forty-five years old is a ripe age for wisdom-filled leaders. Anyone younger cannot be trusted with the leadership of motherland Africa. Such a leadership position is too great a responsibility to be left in the hands of the immature and untested mind.

(c) Of course, birthright. This speaks for itself; one must be a citizen by birth. It is as simple as that. No one should be excluded because of race, culture, tribe, or ethnic background. As long as the birthright is African, that is good enough to be a child of the motherland, and is therefore good enough for a potential leader.

CORNERSTONE INDUSTRY FROM WHICH THE WHOLE CONTINENT WILL SPRING FORWARD

This is a very basic concept, as simple and as fundamental as the foundation of a house being built. These cornerstone industries are:

1. Steel Factories (industry)
2. Concrete Factories
3. Access-ways
4. Agriculture
5. Leadership

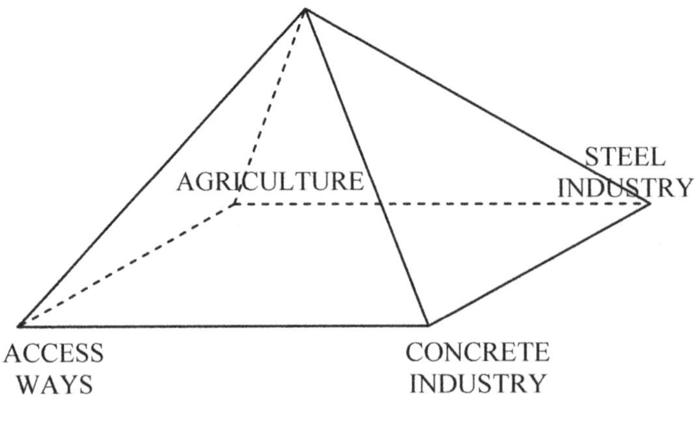

1. The Steel industry. From start to finish, at least four steel factories should be strategically located at each corner of Africa, they will produce the amount of steel needed to build the backbone skeleton structure of the motherland. She must stand tall and erect with the support of her own steel. This steel industry will, in turn, employ thousands of people thereby creating its fair share of an African middle class.
2. The Concrete Industry. This industry will mix and provide all concrete needs. Concrete will become standardized and regulated by industry; in this case, the industry will comprise two or more concrete factories within any area to provide our entire cement and concrete needs. Any nation that has to rely on imported foreign concrete or cement will sooner or later find itself developing at a snail's pace.
3. Access-ways. The next chapter goes into detail on this issue. This is basically the east-west and north-south transcontinental access-ways, all of which should be paralleled by railroads.
4. Agriculture. This speaks for itself. Nothing will happen on an empty stomach; we won't think right, we won't work hard, etc. The agriculture needs have to be addressed even before inception. If a sector of the population has to be allocated the duty of being food providers, then so be it. It has to be done. The motherland cannot sit around and wait for supply and demand to work its way through the system. An amount of land has to be allocated to agriculture, and water, being critical, should be brought to these agricultural lands at the expense of the entire motherland. After all, it is food that will provide the strength to build and grow the entire motherland.
5. Leadership. With a consolidated motherland, this will be the easiest goal to achieve, simply because whoever happens to emerge out of all of Africa as the

leader will be very competent. The process of election that they will have gone through will be training enough for an emerging candidate to qualify as a leader by itself.

TRANSCONTINENTAL ACCESS AND TRANSPORTATION

This is absolutely critical. This is, perhaps, the most critical need of the motherland in its infantile stage. The need for road access is the second most important factor, right behind the actual decision to unify.

Initially, the access-ways have to be built very simply and practically, with a very simple goal of connecting north-south and east-west using the straightest possible routes. These access-ways have to be kept straight; all effort should be made to prevent a snakelike effect on the layout of the access-ways. It is very important to avoid all attempts that seek to connect existing motorways, for multiple reasons:

1) Such roads were not designed with Africation in mind;
2) Existing roads, most likely, are old and poorly maintained, and the cost of refurbishing might be the same as building new roads (or greater);
3) Roads built under Africation will represent a fresh start and a look into the future.

The diagram below attempts to show a proposed layout for the African trans-continental access-ways; potential railroads should be parallel with motorways.

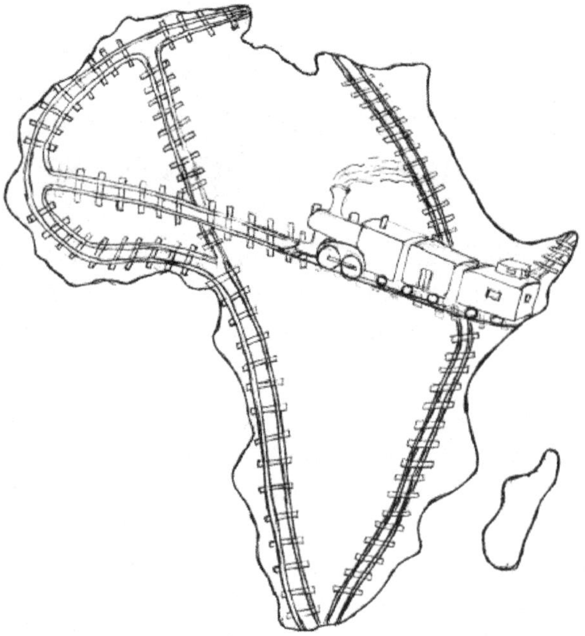

The decision to start construction and the finishing of such roads has to be done in concert with the approval of unification. The implementation of this access-way, from initiation to finish, must be done at lightning speed. Completion of this crucial access-way must be within two years; the time frame is so short because these access-ways will be the lifeline and blood vessels of a newly found economy. The motherland will live or die by these access-ways. Right alongside these access-ways will run parallel railroad tracks for heavy-duty transportation. These must be completed concurrently with the motor access-ways to ensure complete, full, and equal access to the heartland itself. Then, the obvious questions are:

(1) Where will the labor come from;

(2) Where will the heavy machinery come from; and

(3) Where will the steel come from?

Where will the labor come from? Labor in Africa is in abundant supply and is very cheap, particularly unskilled labor. This labor force has to be convinced that it is their patriotic duty, that it is in the future interest of their children, that they participate in this project. Access-way workers, either road or rail, should be granted incentives, such as:

(a) All access-way workers should be paid living wages, to be determined by market forces. The government should oversee and regulate all such labor issues.

(b) The children of access-way workers, regardless of how many there are, should be granted partial scholarships for their educations if they choose to capitalize on this offer. This will be from grade one to university level. Under these conditions, everybody wins. The children, the parents, and the greater African society will benefit from such a project, these access-way builders will not have to worry about their children's educations, this gives them a foot into middle-class Africa. The entire nation wins here, because a percentage of its future generation will be granted higher education access, thereby freeing up those families' limited resources to spend elsewhere within the motherland.

Skilled labor, on the other hand, I believe is available within the continent. This type of labor is a crucial aspect of access-way development. If there is a shortage of skilled access-way workers, then this is one of those few instances where external help ought to be sought after in a very limited amount, simply because on the job training of skilled labor has to be encouraged.

Since completion of the access-ways is a time-sensitive issue, it is imperative that skilled labor is supplemented with extra-African sources if necessary. This will be expensive initially, but that will be the price to pay for completion of the access-ways within a very short period of time.

The alternative is to reinvent the wheel, which might give the illusion of being cheaper, but the reality will be a prolonged access-way construction, thus extending the time which Africa does not have. That time has already been used up by our parents, grandparents, and ancestors.

Where will the heavy machinery come from? Of course, this is that part of the access-way development that is critical but very expensive. To build these access-ways with rapidity, machines such as bulldozers and earthmovers will be needed. At the time of unification, Africa will not be a manufacturer of these heavy-duty machines. However, these machines already exist within the motherland. Perhaps they do not exist in the desired amount or in a centralized entity, such as a company, but for sure: within the status quo of today's Africa, each enclave has a known quantity of bulldozers and trucks that are functional. A stock of what exists today in each nation has to be tabulated. If, at the end of the day, the existing amount is less than the desired amount, then efforts must be made to buy the difference from the international community.

Outright purchase it should be or an outright gift with no strings attached. By all means, loans during the formation of the back-bone structure of the motherland should be avoided. This is because of the value of perception; if effort is made to buy and do for oneself from the onset, then the message being projected outward is one of self-reliance and determination. Besides, it is a good practice to minimize ones debt, or to have no debt, on a newly-formed or starting business venture, in this case it's the United Nations of Africa. (UNA).

By the way, the intent is not to commandeer heavy machinery from its owners, but rather to gain use of the machinery through incentives, keeping in mind the good old proverb that says, "More is achieved with honey than vinegar."

Skeptics will be wondering where the money will come from to buy some of these machines. Well, look around; it will be from two sources that are currently on the markets:

(a) Sales of iron ore, and

(b) Sales of oil.

Where will the steel come from? This will be the skeleton of the entire motherland. If motherland Africa is to succeed and develop, it must first have its own steel mills. The motherland cannot afford to import steel, and besides, the importation of steel has already been done by our parents and grandparents; such has been the practice, and it is still the case, even though it's a proven failure. Today's generation will have to wake up and meet its steel needs. Ore has to be converted into steel within the motherland. A domestic steel industry has to be developed. This is an absolute must, because modern nations are built on the backs of steel beams. Africa cannot afford not to have its own still mills; after all, the mother lode of ore is right here in Africa.

With an appreciation for the value of the steel industry to the motherland, this industry has to be sought after and developed with a dogmatic and unrelenting drive.

The bridges that must form part of the motorways and the steel needed for the rail access-ways must come from these newly formed steel industries; nothing should be imported. Adherence to these guidelines will result in residual benefits, such as:

(1) Homegrown steel suppliers. This speaks for itself; African-owned and African-controlled

suppliers don't have to answer to or ponder about external conditions

(2) It will cut down the cost of production. As the cost of overseas transportation will be virtually eliminated, time wasted waiting for ocean liners to bring steel supplies will be removed, since all production will be local or within the motherland.

The steel industry must be formed by a collaboration of whatever fraction of steel-making capacity or sections is available today within Africa. Africation, at is inception, would be better off if it supports the development of a steel industry that produces twenty units of steel domestically instead of purchasing forty units of steel globally.

The learning curve will be shortened; production capacity will very quickly catch up with global levels. Keeping the learning curve time in mind, any attempt made to continue importing part or all of Africa's steel needs will be counterproductive to the short and long term interest of Africation.

30

IMPORTANCE OF STEEL INDUSTRY

Remember the Stone Age? Well, it's been long gone. It's history, as most people will say. How about the Iron Age? Most would like to believe that is also history, because these are the days of the information age.

Well, the information age of today is just a packaging phenomenon. The information age has always been with us. It was there in the Stone Age, it was there in the Iron Age, and it will be here for whatever ages that will come in the future. This well-packaged information age must be taken in stride, and of course embraced intimately.

The Iron Age, however, is the age of most critical importance to the development of the motherland. Today, all or most of Africa's steel is imported; transportation of heavy metals across the oceans is not cheap. Besides, the vehicles needed to transport these metals are often rented from freight companies of developed nations. All the additional costs are added on to the price of imported steel. The net result is an increase in the actual price of steel and a decrease in the volume of foreign steel that comes by the way of African nations for their home or industrial needs. As a result of these increases in the price of steel, simple industrial development projects, such as bridge constructions, become huge undertakings, to the point where they often exceed the capacity of an entire enclave. These enclaves will ultimately resort to seeking external sources for help, such as the IMF, etc.

Steel is the backbone of any economy. Steel, therefore, must be in plentiful supply and cheap—certainly not as cheap as cement, but it should be quite cheap. After all, the mother lode of ore is right here in the motherland.

An economy that lacks abundant, reasonably-priced steel might as well accept that fact. Such an economy will be stuck in the vicious circle of everlasting development projects that will never fully materialize.

At the beginning of Africation, the steel industry must be among the very first industries to be established. It is the industry that will lift the motherland right out of whatever age it is in right now. Only on the back of steel will the motherland rise.

Establishing African steel production capacity will be a very expensive undertaking. Temptation will be great to acquire funds from extra-Africa sources, but this temptation must be resisted. All cornerstone industries are critical industries; these industries must have their ownership and financial support structure fully embedded within the motherland. If resources are put together all across this motherland, one or two steel factories could be put together. Then, a source of abundant and inexpensive steel would be available right in Africa's backyard, and not across the ocean as it is today.

31

SECURING THE INTEREST OF STEEL-PRODUCING NATIONS

This attempt to form a homegrown steel industry will be met by active and passive resistance globally. This is perhaps the most difficult phase of Africation, simply because steel is big business in all the developed nations. Besides, it is their backbone industry. Faced with these facts, it is only natural for developed nations to move into positions to:

(a) protect their own domestic steel industry, and

(b) ensure that the supply and flow of cheap ore from Africa is not interrupted.

The trick, then, from motherland Africa's side, will be to avoid active resistance from global steel industries. This will only be achieved by fairness to both the needs of the Union and the needs of the developed nations. This balance will be achieved by keeping the ore flowing to developed nations.

The ore must continue flowing. After unification is achieved on paper, extra-African countries receiving African ore should be assured that they will continue to receive and have access to the same source of ore, but at the same time, these receiving nations have to understand that Africa now has its own steel needs, and it's about time she takes matters into her hands. In the immediate aftermath of unification, motherland Africa needs to set up 4 massive steel plants north, south, east and west of the continent. The proportion of ore exported to any individual country will directly relate to the amount of effort that nation has put toward the formation of the motherland's own steel industrial needs. Nations that put zero effort will still get ore, but with restrictions; those that put considerable effort will be granted generous access to ore supply, just as is done today. But of course, under the current trading format, access to ore is given without motherland Africa getting any leverage at the end of the transaction.

Since motherland Africa's steel needs will be for domestic consumption, then it should be honest, comforting, and fair to all steel producing nations. That the Union should give a ten-year assurance and guarantee that she will not participate in the global arena in the direct sales of processed ore (i.e., steel into the international market), such an assurance would give the current steel-producing nations time to position and reposition themselves to accommodate Africa as a future potential player in the global market of steel.

This will also give steel-producing nations the peace of mind that Africa has no intention to flood the international market with cheap steel, thereby having a destabilizing effect. This sounds like a very reasonable proposal; however, all effort must be made to avoid selling the soul of Africa in a long-term contract, like our grandparents did in the past.

On the other hand, if steel-producing nations choose not to support with the equipment and technology needed to establish a domestic steel industry, then the motherland must concentrate its effort, bring together whatever engineers are available, and develop its own steel industry. If the steel produced under Africation is as rudimentary as it was back in the 1800s and 1900s, then so be it. That is where the motherland has to start. After all, these steel industries will not be inventing the wheel; besides, there is plenty of ore within the continent to experiment with, over and over again until we get it right. The steel industry is a crucial industry that the United Nations of Africa (U.N.A) will have to get right, because steel is the backbone of all developed nations.

No nation will develop fully if it lacks the backbone of the steel industry.

Fortunately, the technology to harness steel already exists within Africa today; therefore, it will be up to those capable African nations to take advantage of these virgin market opportunities. Existing steel firms should capitalize on these opportunities to either relocate or expand their operations within the African continent but Africation must happen first.

32

REGULATION AND DIVERSIFICATION OF POWERS

Upon attainment of unification, a structural system and standard of conducting business, both for the government as well as private institutions, should be put into place. The minimum recommended requirements should be:

(1) A large institution, governmental or private, i.e., with a predetermined number of employees, must have boards of directors. These boards of directors should rotate or turn over at least every five years.

(2) Every major company, governmental or private, should be audited. These auditors should be:

 (i) a government auditing body, and

 (ii) a private auditing body

Both auditing bodies should be under two separate boards, and each board should be manned by public members irrespective of their nationalities. Penalties for failure to comply will be put in place; these penalties, however, will not be the main deterrent of corruption, but rather part of the system of checks and balances to regulate the system as it grows.

(3) Fraud control. This will be virtually impossible to bring under absolute control, but greater effort and an ongoing struggle will have to be initiated for fighting fraud.

Therefore, the need for paper trails for all businesses is highly recommended. Businesses will be expected to:

(i) Register with their local government;

(ii) Maintain a documentary trail (paper trail) of their daily transactions. This, however, becomes tricky with regard to businesses whose owners are not educated under such a scenario. Owners who exceed an employee base of greater than five, or revenues greater than a specified amount, must employ an educated clerk to keep a paper trail; otherwise, heavy (but not crippling) penalties shall be levied. The value of paper trails cannot be overstated.

(a) It is important for tax purposes. Societies that are successful usually have very efficient tax collectors.

(b) It facilitates smooth transition in the even of death or illness. Chaos and eventual collapse of a company will be avoided by maintenance of adequate paper trail. Documentation, therefore, is a must for all companies whose employee base is greater than five people.

Long gone should be the days when dad and grandpa conducted business by simply keeping mental records. If the Roman Empire, way back then, (27 BC) was able to keep good records of their dealings and had efficient tax collection systems, I see no reason why modern day Africa cannot do any better.

A successful future for Africa will depend on how well organized the system is. Those societies that are highly organized have proven to be the successful countries. If

Africa is to follow suit, then it must start to get its ducks in a row by stressing the need for proper paper trails in all commercial ventures, regardless of size.

With Africation will come standardization of all tax collecting mechanisms as well as bookkeeping methods. Thousands will be employed from all across Africa. Periodic reshuffling of tax collectors and accountants from east to west, north to south and vice versa will become an effective corruption fighting tool, as personnel will be rotated before they establish the roots of corruption.

NATIONAL DEFENSE

These are very conservative numbers; the benefit of the doubt is given to each individual country.

African Countries, Population, and Uniformed Armed Forces		
Country	Population (in millions)	Armed Forces (in thousands)
Algeria	30.4	125
Angola	10.8	110
Benin	6.1	5
Botswana	1.4	9
Burkina Faso	12	10
Burundi	5.5	46
Cameron	15	21
Cape Verde	0.4	1
C. Africa	3.3	4
Chad	7.3	28
Comoros	0.54	
R. Congo	2.6	10
Cote D'Ivoire	15.4	13
D. Congo (Zaire)	55	80
Djibouti	0.44	9
Egypt	66.0	440
Equatorial Guinea	0.45	1
Eritrea	3.8	90
Ethiopia	58	170

Gabon	1.2	5
Gambia	1.2	1
Ghana	18	7
Guinea Conakry	7.6	10
Guinea Bissau	1.2	8
Kenya	21	24
Lesotho	2.2	2
Liberia	2.7	5
Libya	5.6	75
Madagascar	16	13
Malawi	9.5	5
Mali	10	7
Mauritania	2.5	15
Mauritius	1.5	
Morocco	29.1	360
Mozambique	18.6	10
Namibia	1.6	9
Niger	9.6	5
Nigeria	130	80
Rwanda	7.9	75
Sao Tome & Principe	0.150	
Senegal	10	10
Seychelles	0.78	
Sierra Leone	5	5
Somalia	6.8	1
South Africa	30.9	60
Sudan	33.5	115
Swaziland	0.99	3
Tanzania	30.6	108
Togo	4.9	9
Tunisia	9.3	33
Uganda	22	55
Zambia	9.4	20
Zimbabwe	11	41
TOTAL	**800 mil**	**2.1 mil**

With regard to the security and defense of the motherland, I must say right off the bat that am not an expert on this issue. However, having studied so much of global history and current major conflicts all over the world, I have come to the conclusion that supremacy—especially air supremacy—in the form of offensive capability belongs to the highly industrialized nations.

Africa, as a whole, would not be able to intercept any challenges to its air space effectively. Therefore, the motherland is forced into the position of defending its home and position.

Defense is important, but it is not an immediate priority; besides, I do not foresee any potential enemy for the motherland in the near future. When we say defense, we mean absolute, 100% defense to the bones, with zero offensive capability. This is simply because airplanes, jet fighters, etc. are all very expensive. Besides, motherland Africa lacks the infrastructure to manufacture such sophisticated machines, which therefore means that in order to acquire such machines, they would have to be purchased from external sources. This, in turn, would mean that the motherland would be getting whatever the seller wants to sell. What the motherland cannot make, with regard to war machinery, she must not buy; the reality is that if the motherland has to buy weapons, she is already a two-time loser.

1) The best will be kept for the seller themselves. Only second-class machinery would be available for purchase.
2) These machines are not cheap. Precious resources are needed, and they could be used elsewhere.

Antiaircraft missiles, on the other hand, are much cheaper, and could be made and improved upon right here within the motherland. Millions could be manufactured, yes, millions of them. Yes, antiaircraft missiles, not those outdated World War II tracers; what I mean is sophisticated antiaircraft that has all the capability to engage and intercept uninvited guests as high up into the heavens as aircraft can fly. The same philosophy should apply to the coastal defense, both at sea level and under the sea.

With regard to nuclear weapons, the motherland should opt to keep the continent nuclear free; after all, the motherland is only interested in defending and not destroying her children or homeland.

This attitude and approach to defense should only be considered five to ten years into unification. Setting the cornerstone industries in motion is more of a priority initially than defense is. Defense should be a second phase structural design in unification. That is as much as I can talk about on this topic, because again, I will admit that I don't know much about this.

However, under the current status quo of Africa's defense, there is no such thing as Africa's defense. Each enclave has its armed forces well contained within their borders. At the same time, there are no true alliances or cooperation among these enclaves.

In today's Africa, 2.1 million armed soldiers roam the motherland. That makes Africa the largest standing army in the world. On paper, that sounds very impressive; it sounds like Africa is a formidable foe, but the actual reality is that these 2.1 million is not any more formidable than the strongest enclave within the continent. This collective weakness in total military capability is due to the compartmentalization of the continent as it is today.

Under Africation, there lies the potential to combine the entire military capability of the motherland. This act alone will result in numerous positive side effects, such as:

1) Concentration of resources under centralized control. This allows for the formation of better defense strategies for the entire motherland. The decision to mobilize could be made faster, and would be easier to implement.

2) Africation conserves on all military resources, both in terms of human personnel as well as hardware; under Africation, two million armed soldiers could be reduced to one million or fewer. With regard to hardware, unnecessary duplication and reduplication of the same absolute hardware will be minimized.

3) The armed forces will emerge as an industrial complex instead of just another entity within an enclave and so within the motherland. As an industrial complex, employment opportunities will open up for engineers and corporations that supports such complexes.

4) With consolidated armed forces, there lies the end of the frequent civil wars of Rwandas, Somalias, Sierra Leones, and the likes of them. Such wasteful negative energy that exists today within the status quo enclaves will be channeled into positive action for timely intervention in future Rwandas.

Africa's enemies in this generation and the next will not be foreign invaders, foreign air fleets, or foreign armadas.

The enemies of Africa are mostly foot soldiers, at best fleets of SUVs, packed to capacity with local thugs. This is the direction Africa's defense should be geared toward and prepared to confront.

These thugs in SUVs have inflicted devastating blows to multiple African countries, such as Sierra Leone, Ivory Coast, Somalia, etc.

Unless the entire defense resource of the motherland is consolidated to face such internal demons, motherland Africa will continue to see its enclaves overrun by thugs at a regular interval of every five years. All it takes to set a country back forty years is six months of anarchy; the math is not in Africa's favor.

What good are all those mighty military generals and their armies, the air forces and naval fleets within the motherland?

So far, they have proven to be insignificant in the greater arena of their own motherland. What positive value have the current armies contributed to the situation in Sudan? Much credit should be given to their role in Sierra Leone; such performance should serve as a poster child for the AU at its best. That is a model against which all future conflict resolution should be measured.

However, the inability to duplicate such success in Sudan highlights the fundamental design flaw built in the status quo of fragmented Africa. With all of its enclaves acting independently of each other, Sudan highlights the problem associated with the lack of a group function; that is what Africation is all about.

Yes, it's true that Sudan is the largest country in Africa, but Sudan's population is only forty million. That is about one-twentieth the population of Africa. Besides, Sudan's army is not a first class world army; she might be a tough nut to crack, but certainly not too tough for the collective might of Africa.

Knowing the strength of Sudan's military capability, logic and reasoning cannot explain away the inability of the entire motherland to intervene and remedy the decade-old problems of Sudan. The usual excuse for the lack of military hardware does not hold here, for many reasons.

i) Sudan's military does not have the numbers to take on any significant coalition of African countries. The math, therefore, is in favor of the greater motherland.

ii) Lack of hardware is an old excuse. Such reasoning does not hold ground any longer; even if there was a total lack of transportation to take African Union solders to battlefield Sudan, history has shown that greater distances have been covered on foot under much tougher conditions. If Union soldiers had to make the journey on foot, they would still get there on time. After all, the situation in Sudan has been going on for over ten years now. It will not take ten years to reach Sudan from any corner of the motherland, nor do I propose for African Union soldiers to get there on foot.

The obvious reason for such a lack of collective will and drive is due to the fragmented states in which we are today. The desire, will, and drive would have been much easier to achieve and control under Africation.

iii) As mentioned earlier, Sudan's armed forces are not those of a first world nation. Therefore, all that is needed in terms of firearms are already right here within each enclave. The call for airplanes from the west by AU generals is simply a smokescreen to mask the inherited design flaws in the African Union.

Help from extra-African countries is reluctant help; such help is help that is slow to come. The actual reality is that this help has been coming less and less frequently. When they do come, they are often much too late, i.e., Rwanda, Liberia, Sierra Leone, Sudan, etc. Often, by the time help arrives, the ailing enclave is already set back more than forty years.

One can't fault extra-African countries for not rushing to send their sons and daughters to die in Africa; why should they? After all, they don't have a dog in the fight. Africans have dogs in the fight. African people must fight these battles when and where they crop up from the very beginning. Failure to do so will simply result in postponing the fight for a later day; by that later day, the fight will be right at your doorsteps. What then? Join the line and wait for extra-African help?

Unless Africa realizes that these thugs on SUVs are the enemies within (today it is Sudan, for sure, but within the next five years it will be somewhere else, perhaps Guinea, perhaps Congo, Nigeria, Zimbabwe, no one knows), one thing is for sure: anarchy could come to your peaceful enclave. Don't fool yourself and make believe it may not happen. Surely our grandpas in Sierra Leone never saw it coming. Likewise, the people of Ivory Coast did not see it coming either.

Knowing the obvious, that the demon is within and she will occasionally rise from within, it is the duty and responsibility of the collective African society to be able to handle such security or defense issues swiftly and efficiently from among its own people, not from extra-African nations. Africation, therefore, is a wise remedy for any potential anarchy.

34

RELIGION AND THE MOTHERLAND

This is a topic that is very difficult to tackle. It is very uncomfortable for most people to deal with. It's is a topic in which everyone has his or her own biases that are brought along whenever this issue is being dealt with. Knowing this as a fact of human behavior, religious tolerance guidelines should be put in place from the onset of Africation. These guidelines will serve to mediate between religions.

Two obvious religions seems to be dominant on the African landscape.

1) Muslims, and
2) Christians.

These two religions, therefore, must be acknowledged equally in the Constitution of the motherland. They must carry equal weight and time in any governmental gathering or document.

- No religion should be given preference over the other.
- Leaders, or any public African officials who use religion to incite the people against each other, should be dealt with appropriately. Their punishments must have teeth.
- There should be a national religious advisory body made up of equal number of Christian and Muslim, they will mediate minor conflicts among all faiths.

- Biblical and Islamic laws cannot be passed onto nonbelievers; these laws must not cross faiths. They must only apply to themselves and not to others of different faiths.
- There should be zero tolerance to religious inciters or instigators.
- Other preventative guidelines against religious uprisings should be put into place from the very onset at Africation.
- With regard to the other, smaller religions, these must be tolerated, but cannot be accommodated equally like Christian and Muslim faith. These smaller religions and faiths are part of the greater African community; though they are smaller, these smaller groups have to be given full protection and rights to express and exercise themselves within their motherland. Under no situation should any of the bigger religious groups impose their will upon or intimidate such smaller groups.
- Again, zero tolerance should be the case for such religious misbehaviors. Failure to enforce this part of the religious guidelines would be catastrophic; we have all seen what our brothers and sisters are capable of doing in the name of religion.
- Religion is a delicate issue, as delicate as nitroglycerin. It must be handled delicately, and the people have to be constantly reminded of its explosive potential. Therefore, religion in a unified motherland must be treated with respect at all times. The importance of the potential explosive nature of religion cannot be over emphasized.
- Very important religious gatherings between the unified government and the two main religions have to happen. There, the guidelines should be put in place. During those guideline meetings, minor

religious groups should not participate, because their interest will be represented by the unified government. Inclusion of minor religious groups during the guideline meetings will only serve to water down the potency of any guidelines.

35

FOREIGN INVESTMENTS

This simply means the infusion of foreign ideas and foreign monies. I happen to see nothing wrong with such investments. In fact, such investments should be encouraged. There is no such thing as a free ride; foreign investors must pay their fair and equal share of taxes to the motherland.

These investors will contribute to the building of the motherland in many ways, such as:

(i) They will build and add on to the visual infrastructure through the factories or office buildings that they will have to erect in order to do business;

(ii) They will have to employ locals, thereby providing a very valuable contribution to the development of the middle class;

(iii) They will provide a source of tax revenue, and this is revenue coming from outside the motherland;

(iv) They will bring along with them a different view and foreign technology—in other words, a view from outside the box; and

(v) In the event that some of the foreign investors decide to leave or go back home to their own homelands, the motherland will gain, because infrastructural developments that have been made cannot be packed up into a suitcase and taken

> along with those foreign investors. These, therefore, are left behind.

Therefore, never nationalize these industries, because that will be the loss of the goose that lays the golden eggs.

The only exception to massive foreign investments is the cornerstone industries. One such industry is the steel industry. Until the continent is developed, this industry must lie under the full control of domestic ownership, because the goal then, is all about accessible prices and volume, as discussed in the chapter on steel.

36

FOREIGN AID OR TRADE PARTNERS

As discussed in the Forbidden Fruit chapter, much of the economy of the motherland has become wrapped around the phrase “foreign aid.” In the tiny West African country of Gambia, up to 45% of the GDP of that country depends on foreign aid. This is certainly too huge a sector of its economy to be dependent on the benevolence of foreign donor. In discussing this, what comes to my mind is the old adage “give a man a fish, you feed him for a day, but teach him how to fish, you feed him for a lifetime.” The donors are not going to teach us how to fish, because even putting selfishness aside; it is just not in their interest to do so.

The fact is that nothing comes for free in this world, and there is no free lunch anywhere. There is always going to be some consideration in exchange for any aid given. In the days where we had bipolar world structures, foreign aid was given in exchange for the recipients aligning themselves with the ideology of one of the superpowers. In those days, we could at least play one power against the other, although those politics were destructive; in large part, those politics led to the destabilization of much of the motherland, culminating in many coups, counter coups d’état, and civil wars, the effects of which we are still seeing . These days however, with the obliteration of the former Soviet Union, we simply do not have that luxury. The only way in which we can get out of the liability zone and make the motherland a major global economic player, and indeed fight to defeat poverty is through trade. As Governor Bush, now President Bush rightly said in his fall 2000 campaign, “Africa is not a foreign policy priority for the United States." I believe he was and still is right, although much has changed since then. My dear brothers and sisters of the motherland, as President Reagan once said (and no harm meant here), "Africa must pick itself up by its bootstraps." Some would say it is an insult, but I say it is a wake up call. What must we do? I don't want to get too philosophical; otherwise, I would have gone down the road of getting rid of selfishness, nepotism, greed, and so on and so forth, but that gives us few answers to the problem at hand. So I will say: let's get to work. I remember the 1970s, when Gambia devalued its currency for the first time, and we had to go through major economic restructuring. Our then President, Sir Dawda Jawara, in preparing the nation for this major economic blow, came up with a philosophy called "tesito" in Mandingo. It simply means self-help, self-reliance, and self-sufficiency. It was an excellent idea, but like many African leaders since post colonial, he was swimming up stream against a flawed African system which meant failure was inevitable.

This idea is what Africa, collectively, as a single unit, needs to revisit if she wants to become a force to be reckoned with. So now what must we do?

Firstly, we must move away from the idea of dependency on foreign aid. We all know Africa is a continent rich with natural resources; that is an undisputed fact, but on the other hand, we all know in fiscal matters Africa is a very poor continent. That is also an undisputed fact. In the motherland, we have all sorts of natural resources, from the almighty oil to the terrifying and scary uranium. At least four of the other seven continents on this earth are not as rich in resources as Africa. The question is: why is Africa still lagging behind the rest?

Back in the 1970s, just after independence, and I must say that ironically, after freeing ourselves from the tyranny of colonialism, the rates of exchange for most of the currencies in the motherland was one-to-one. In other words, they were at equal power with the US dollar. My mother used to receive a publication, from what I believe was a religious charity called “NOW,” in which people were always asking for help for the desperately poor kids in Singapore and the Far East. Today, thirty years later, the tables have turned. Singapore is almost a first world economy in its own right, with a top tier per capita income—in fact, it is one of the highest in the world. They did this within three decades, with almost no natural resources except for the desire to succeed and a leadership filled with passion and resolve. That is what we need to succeed in the motherland, and everyone has a role to play. We owe it to ourselves, to our posterity, and to our children to make Africation a reality. In order to achieve this, some sacrifices have to be made; the good old proverb says, “no pain, no gain.” If the African enclaves do not make the sacrifice and Africate now, there will certainly be no gains later.

Secondly: African enclaves must approach trade through economic integration, with an emphasis on imports and exports, not only exports of raw materials, but of finished products, besides, 850 million people is a large enough market that is capable of sustaining any African industry. All of which will help to improve the standard of living for all Africans.

By now, one should gather that when talking about finished products, I am referring to the manufacturing sector. No viable economy can survive by importing 100% of its population’s everyday needs, even with the highest per capita income and the best foreign reserves. Such a nation will go broke because of a lopsided economy and trade imbalances. Moreover, in strengthening our manufacturing sector, if we are to achieve economies of scale, our primary target should be our local market. The motherland currently has close to or more than one billion people. We most certainly have the market. The strongest economy in the world has a local market of just half that. We certainly have the potential to be better.

Going back to trade, it is only through economic integration that it is possible to achieve economies of scale, and for those smaller territories in the motherland, the only way to break out is through integration. African territories like Gambia, Niger, Cape Verde Island, Lesotho, and Madagascar, to name a few, cannot break out of the liability zone except through integration. Some may argue that if Taiwan and Singapore could liberate themselves economically, then why can't we? But my answer is that, given the current geopolitical and socioeconomic conditions of all African states at this time, integration will certainly be better and much easier.

Thirdly: It is a disgrace to the motherland that we trade with every other country in the world except with each other. It is also a shame that transcontinental infrastructure is nonexistent. Traveling by road or rail within today's Africa is an extremely difficult endeavor; traveling by air is not great, but it is manageable, especially when the funds are there. Traveling by road is a priority that has been ignored. Such a road should have been put in place immediately after independence; it's now forty to fifty years since then, but yet Africa is still stuck in the same predicament as she was during her pre-independence days.

It takes six hours to travel by road from Dakar to Banjul, a distance of half the miles from Washington, D.C. to Norfolk, Virginia, (under 200 miles), and it takes an average of five days to post an ordinary mail from Banjul to Dakar. Transcontinental railroad is almost zero.

For those Africans quick to make excuses for the lack of such roads or rail access-ways by rehashing the usual one liner 'lack of funds', perhaps as a refresher they ought to consider the Great Wall of China. This 4000 miles wall was built way back in the 220s BC, with inferior technology, with less money, yes with less money; with inferior material, and finally under much more treacherous conditions than those present in Africa today. Thus we search for the answer to the question, if China then can do it then what is holding 21st century Africa. Africation, as argued earlier, is the only way out of the modern day mud in which Africa is stuck. The world has now become one big village. If Africa, does not reposition itself to play an active role in the economic and geopolitical activities in this village, then Africans will continue to live at the mercy of the other cohabitants. Therefore, it is important that Africation becomes a reality in the very near future.

The free movement of people and goods, if I could borrow one of the catch phrases of ECOWAS (a sub-regional African organization), is absolutely vital to our economic development. Such free movement was promised way back in 1975.

Finally: For trade, we must have access to the global market. In other words, we must tap into the phenomenon of globalization, because Africa does not want to remain in a state of self pity; Africa wants to move to self sufficiency. Therefore, it is important that our markets be opened to foreign participation with the least government interference possible. An open market economy has many imperfections, but it is now proven to be one of the systems that can lift people out of poverty and raise their standards of living. Through Africation, African-based companies will have the large, African market to perfect their products and marketing strategies before making the ultimate leap into the global arena.

IMPLEMENTATION

37

GRASSROOTS MOVEMENT

Africation has to be a grassroots movement; this movement must come from the people themselves, not from the governments. If we wait for the governments to initiate unification, then unification will never be achieved; otherwise, the OAU would have taken us there, or the AU would be taking us there by now. Besides, unification is contrary to the immediate interest of most governments; after all, why should they give up the goose that lays the golden eggs? Hence, the grassroots movements and the involvement of folks from the entire African landscape is important, from:

- East to West and North to South,
- The primary schools to high schools, colleges and universities.
- Working class folks and all kinds of able-bodied folks.

African people will have to mobilize in numbers and frequency. Without such a movement, I see no other realistic path to unification. A series of peaceful marches for Africation movement has to be started.

These march date will be synchronized with scheduled march dates in other African nations in order to have the most impact. These march dates must be frequent, repetitive, and continue; come rain, shine, or bullets, the march must go on.

Once this grassroots movement has started to take place all over the motherland, the support of the existing governments will fall into place, and they will give that support to their people.

This support from the governments will be there, because even among the most corrupt and ruthless people in governments, their subconscious and inner selves long for the day of a United Nations of Africa (U.N.A). Besides, their love for the motherland is greater than their selfish needs. Hence, we can count on the eventual support of all governments.

But first, the people must push for it. The march must start, and the march must go on until we get there.

38

THE WAY FORWARD TO UNIFICATION

In an ideal world, it would be beautiful, romantic, wonderful, marvelous, and so on, to have the enclaves next to each other unify, regionally at first, then move on to interregional unification. But this is not an ideal world; consequently we will have to take unification in whatever from it comes.

In a hypothetical scenario, if Guinea, Libya, and Mozambique buy into this Africation idea, then these three countries will be pioneers. Though they are geographically separated, geography in this case should be disregarded. The African enclaves, collectively, are siblings; they all share the same motherland Africa. Sibling blood spreads wider than geography, so unification under these circumstances must go ahead with everyone's blessing. In the long run, the dots or gaps between these pioneers will be connected.

= Countries in between the pioneer countries that are not yet ready to make the faithful leap of Africation.

= Pioneer Countries. They have started the march forward. These are the first few countries that recognize the value of Africation, and they have made the ultimate commitment to the unification of motherland Africa.

These hypothetical pioneer countries and their leaders will secure themselves a place in African modern history. This time, it will be a written history. They will, for the first time, be doing something for their people beyond what their minds can dream of, beyond what they can touch, and of course beyond their domain.

As for those dots that need to be connected, they should not be shunned by the pioneer countries. They should instead be loved with the love a big brother gives to his younger brother. These dotted countries will always be welcome to join the Union, but while they remain dotted, they ought to be left on their own to continue enjoying the disadvantages that the status quo has been offering them all these years. Pioneer countries must not offer to share incentives with the dotted enclaves; such incentives are for members only.

To simplify my point, with the younger brother analogy, no advice or warning will keep him straight. If you leave that brother out in the real world for a year or two, he will sooner or later begin to appreciate the advice and support given by the older brother after the world has taught him a lesson or two. The same will have to apply between the dotted and the pioneer countries.

After these hypothetical pioneer countries have started the ball rolling, it will be very important to have short timeline goals. These goals must be adhered to.

By short timeline goals, we mean intervals measured in months and not years. Because the fruit of the harvest has to be eaten, or at least tasted, by those who planted them, the theory of planting seeds and not enjoying the harvest is an old African theory that has proven to be a failure in both our parents' era and our grandparents' era. Everything that our parents and grandparents have grown for us has turned out to be inadequate in today's modern times.

Therefore, the value of very short timelines is important to the psyches of those who make the sacrifice; these same folks should be able to see and taste the fruits of their labors. That taste in their mouths, their minds, and their souls will be a thirst-quenching incentive for them to continue sowing the seeds of Africation and development for the future generations.

CATALYST OF UNIFICATION IS BY A MOVEMENT OF THE PEOPLE

Unification has to come as a movement of the nations. A movement of nations does not happen by itself, nor will it happen with the approval or blessing of any heads of state or governments.

The people have to mobilize with a common goal that demands for unification of motherland Africa. A mobilized nation has momentum; a nation on the move cannot be derailed, because the movement of the people will continue on track.

This movement, therefore, has to be a grassroots movement, from high schools, to colleges and universities, to the very young working class. For those in the older working class, only their blessing is asked for.

This movement is about the future with an emphasis on the future. It is not about today; today, it's obvious that the status quo has failed us. A complete overhaul of the status quo is therefore required.

Speaking of unification and dreaming about it will not bring it about. The people have to want it, the people have to demand it, the people have to pursue it, and the people have to live through it.

A "Hakuna Matata," or a no problem attitude, will only serve to maintain the status quo. For those who are skeptical, they need not look back too far into the history books. Just look back to the eighties and nineties. There, you will find two reasons to discount and ignore all skeptics:

(1) The Soviet Union, by all accounts, was a much more powerful country in all aspects of its society than any of the existing African governments individually or collectively. But yet the people mobilized themselves and thus, were able to stand up to it and change the course of their future. Such was also the case with Poland.

(2) South Africa. Remember the all-powerful apartheid regime? It was strong enough to take the entire continent collectively. Yet sure enough, it was brought to its knees by—you guessed it—high school students. High school students did them in.

With the above examples as a point of reference, the logical conclusion is that a nation on the move is in motion because of the movement of its people.

Movement by the people can only be stopped by the people themselves; no external force, no matter how powerful, can stop such a movement.

The future of the motherland, therefore, is in your hands. People of Africa, you must take your future into your own hands and shape that future, or sit idly by and watch some foreign nation shape a future for you, your children, your grandchildren and your nation through their offices of foreign affairs or foreign policies. Yes, inaction has consequences. These consequences are always undesirable and demoralizing to the people, their nations, and the entire continent; worst of all, foreign policies put in place by foreign nations have a gravitational pull on the motherland's dreams, which have so far been kept locked up tight in a bottle, pulling them where the foreign policies of extra-African nations believe the motherland's dreams ought to be.

The call to arms among real estate developers is "build it and they will come." The same applies to Africa. Build it, Africate to a viable market, and they will come along with the investment train. No true investor or capitalist will sit by and watch the Africation train go by instead of participating; that would be contrary to the fundamental belief of capitalism.

Our call to arms is "Africation." African people, irrespective of their global locations, must express and show their demand for Africation collectively and simultaneously.

PATH TO CONSOLIDATION IS SOLIDARITY BUT NOT REVOLUTION

Revolution has always been associated with change. There were the Russian, the French, and the American Revolutions. These were all revolutions that were appreciated by the people of their times and are immortalized by today's generation. Today in Africa, we have either seen or heard about too many revolutions.

Revolution in Africa means rebels, coups d'état, genocides, death, and the destruction of our fragile cities, often resulting in some ill-prepared leader with a gun emerging and forcing the masses into submission under their trigger-happy hands.

The word revolution, therefore, is an absolute no-no. Up and down, the continent is dotted by multiple ruthless government agencies, but Poland, only a few years ago, had an even more ruthless government. In the 80s, if Lech Wałęsa was able, under those conditions, to organize and bring about Solidarność to Poland, then surely solidarity with an African touch should work for the motherland.

Any African who has the ability to read and comprehend this article should be ready to make the sacrifice. With Africation, the people become the weapons of revolution. This will be a peaceful war with no enemies in sight, not even governments or government agencies. It will be a fight against the self-centered nature of the African man or African woman. It will be a revolution that seeks to bring out the group interest ahead of self interest.

Going down the path of the traditional revolution, with guns and machetes, etc., is contrary to the interest of Africa's solidarity. That type of war limits the number of boots on the ground. Only the young, aggressive, and violent can participate in a traditional war, but with solidarity, all can participate—even the old and the sick. Besides, going down the path of revolution will provide the pretence that extra-African forces need to intervene on a humanitarian basis. Therefore, total separation from the word "revolution" will make any consolidation effort more politically correct, palatable, and pacifying to all extra-African sectors of this world. Revolution, therefore, is an absolute no. Solidarity is the key word; "solidarity for Africation" should be the phrase.

41

WORKING TOWARD A FEDERATION

We should know from the start that Africation will not be an easy process. There will be many bumps and hurdles, but like all other countries that have gone through a similar process, Africa should be able to prevail at the end of the day—if the people of Africa have the will and resolve to see Africation through.

The Federal government shall consist of three arms, namely, the Legislature, the Executive, and the Judiciary. The Legislature shall consist of two chambers; in other words, it shall be bicameral, and it shall consist of the House and the Senate. The lower house will be made up of proportional representation, which means that the total members for any one particular state will depend on that state's population. This should not be static, since we now have people moving freely from state to state, and the movement of people and population growth can be affected by various factors, many of which are controllable. Some states will initially outnumber others in the lower house for obvious reasons, but that should not be permanent; this should balance out in the upper house, where each state should have equal representation. Their terms will be determined by the experts who will draft these rules. Both houses together will be responsible for all federal laws. For any bill to become law, both houses will have to legislate their own version of the same bill, meet in conference to reconcile the two versions, and work out compromises whenever there are differences before sending a completed bill to the President's desk for his signature.

The President shall, however, have a veto power, which can be overridden by a two-thirds majority in each Legislative house. There will be a limit to the number of legislators in the lower house, and in the upper house, regardless of size, each state shall have two representatives. The number of legislators in the lower house shall decrease or increase per state, depending on population growth or shrinkage. The Judiciary also has the power to declare a law null and void if the matter is brought before it by any aggrieved persons or group; however, it can only challenge its constitutionality. There should be regular election in each of the chambers at a fixed date yearly, and this will be enshrined in the Constitution. The term limits for each chamber will also be enshrined in the Constitution. Suspension of election will be a rarity except in certain unavoidable circumstances, and this will be restricted to a county or a state; it will never happen to the Union as a whole. The date for elections will be stipulated in the Constitution, and on this day, all elections—County, State, and Federal—will be held. Term limits for Senators and Representatives will be stipulated in the rules governing the two chambers. The languages for business will be English, French and Arabic.

Further details will be worked out by others who are better informed on this issue than we are.

THE TRANSITION

Where do we start on this thorny topic? Well, let's see. We still have the dysfunctional Organization of African Unity, now called the African Union. That looks like a good place to start; at least we have the framework already. But let's see, looking around the world, I believe the best workable example of a federation or Union is the United States.

I know critics and skeptics may argue that we in Africa are so different from the social composition of the United States that if we copy their system of federation, we will be doomed to failure from the start. But let's pause and look at what we have in common. If nothing else, we do have a strong desire to be at least as economically prosperous as they are. That's a good place to start. Beside even the United States copied most of its political systems from the Roman Empire.

I believe that we do not have the time or the luxury of inventing a totally new system, when we have one that we can try. At least we know that it has worked somewhere. Besides, these critics have to start making their arguments in a public forum; by doing so, it gives others the same opportunities to be equally critical. Now, let's see, where can we start? We once dealt with the question of sovereignty.

We on the continent of Africa love our independence, and we love nationalism, but we have lost much of our sovereignty to internationalism because of our indifference. If only we were able, as a continent, to commit ourselves to the stronger ideals of the first two concepts, mainly democracy and federalism, we would regain much of the political and economic sovereignty we lost to internationalism.

Let's start with democracy. Sir Winston Churchill once said, "Democracy is the craziest form of government except for all others." Yes, it does have its imperfections, but from history, it's the most reliable form of government. Therefore, if any state in the motherland wants to join the Union, they must commit to democracy and a representative form of government. All military and pseudo-military forms of government, as well as dictatorships, must cease and give way to genuine, non-controversial elections. Initially, however, Africation remains committed to the idea of leaving the existing governments in place with immunity for five years after unification.

Elections should begin at the local level. There should be considerable power given to the local governments, where their spheres of influence do not conflict with the state or federal governments, and this should be the same for the relationship between the federal and state governments.

Each government wanting to join the Union should be willing to revisit its constitution. There should be a referendum held in that state, testing the will of the people to join. The second stage is rewriting the state constitution to reflect a broad outline, which should be drafted by a panel of constitutional experts. After the state constitution has been ratified, then local elections can take place. Then, after this step, we move into the statewide elections mode, where we create the Arms of Government at the State level. The current heads of state will be downgraded to governors, and they must have a bicameral legislature.

The Judiciary may reflect the cultural practices of each state at the lower levels, but must be based on constitutional and common law practices at the upper echelons. I don't see the reason why judges would run for office, but if they do, it should be on the same platform as the Executive and

Legislative arms. Otherwise, they could be appointed by the Executive, with advice and consent or input from one of the houses, preferably the Senate, since it will have equal representation form each region, district, or county in the state.

Once this is done, the state is ready to move into the Union. There should be free movement of people and goods between each state, and all trade barriers should be lifted. Travel documents will be federalized to reflect the new status of the citizens; in other words, they should have adopted a free market economy. I know this is not a flawless system, but it has been proven to be the most reliable way to give people the "good life," in which everybody gets a fair shot at cracking the nut of prosperity. After this, they shall enter the Union. I might add that the timeframe to implement this transition must be very short, because no condition is permanent; things can change very quickly. The idea of African unification is already forty years late, so all plans to go through this process must be done quickly. We don't want more everlasting development plans.

43

THE EXECUTIVE

The Executive branch will be headed by the President. He will have a running mate at the time of his election, who may succeed him in the event of his resignation, incapacitation, or death. The Vice President may choose to run for office at the end of the President's term of office.

The President will be in charge of the day-to-day administration of the Union. To assist him, he will have a team of Cabinet members, and their designation will be Secretaries of State. The appointment of these men and women shall be the Presidents prerogative. They may come from any walk of life, but they must be confirmed by the Senate on an up or down vote. Should one be rejected, he could then appoint someone else. Cabinet members shall not be members of the Legislature or the Judiciary at the time of their confirmation by the Senate.

The President shall also appoint non-cabinet officers to help him with other distractive duties, and the Constitution will determine whether they require Senate confirmation. As aforementioned, the President shall have veto powers on legislation, which can be overridden by a two-thirds majority in both houses. It will also be the President's responsibility to appoint federal judges.

The President is responsible for and will conduct and determine the foreign policy of the Union. However, all treaties will need Senate ratification for them to become law.

44

THE FEDERAL JUDICIARY

Appointment to the federal bench shall be the prerogative of the President. The Senate, however, shall have an advisory and approval role. If a nominee of the President is not confirmed, the President must withdraw the nomination and nominate someone else.

Federal appointments are for life, and once one is appointed, he or she cannot be removed from office by the Executive. The Constitution shall stipulate the grounds and processes for the termination of a Judicial appointment.

The hierarchy of the court shall consist of the trial, appellate, and Supreme Court. The Chief Justice of the Supreme Court shall be the head of the Judiciary.

45

PURPOSE AND CONCLUSION OF THIS BOOK

Having heard all the excuses and reasons for the current feeble condition of all enclaves within this continent, it is our belief and intention to concentrate the systemic pathologies within Africa into this handbook. This concentration will focus our thoughts, giving us a good understanding of these pathologies, their true causes, and the potential options available for alleviating and remedying Africa's situation.

With the disposal of communism, capitalism emerges as the sole dominant doctrine in these modern times. These are, therefore, favorable times for the cultivation of Africation. These times are favorable due to:

1) An absence of countervailing forces. As long as Africation adapts the proven system of capitalism for its comprehensive unification plan, then I foresee no gathering clouds against Africation in the near or distant future of the motherland.
2) A critical mass of educated elite now exists within the motherland, and this mass will continue to grow, as opposed to what happened in the times of our parents and grandparents
3) Experience is a great teacher. Africa has seen its role, position, and plight in this global arena relegated to one of insignificancy and disgrace. There is no substitute for the value of such an experience; past, present, and potential future experiences should be adequate to activate and

motivate all enclaves and their citizens to start this unification process with a vengeance, to stop clowning around about this regional mumbo-jumbo. Regionalization, as discussed earlier, is simply another delaying tactic, just like the good old O.A.U, now the A.U. Enclaves interested in unification must and will have to bypass AU eternal, gradualistic approach and adapt a more realistic path to transition. Once again, the goal is not only to achieve unification within our lifetimes, but also to achieve it within the shortest possible time.

4) The argument to act now for the preservation of resources. Some resources have been lost for good; the motherland will never get them back. The resources that are left should be preserved and utilized for the betterment of the entire motherland. There comes a time in life when decisions have to be made. Even the failure to make a decision is considered a decision, so the time has come for all existing enclaves and their citizens to decide what type of African they are. Like my professor used to say, "There are 3 types of people in this world;" the same applies to Africa. There are 3 types of Africans:

    (a) Those who sit idly and watch things happen;
    (b) Those who make things happen; and
    (c) Those who do not know what the hell happened even if it hits them in the face.

The lines are drawn; the world has drawn the lines. Africa has to start making things happen, or let others control her destiny for good. The global wheel of progress is in motion; it will not stop for any nation, not even for poor continental Africa. Africa can either rotate with it or be rotated whichever way it chooses, she will be rotated.

GLOSSARY

AFRICATION: The process of formation of a unified Africa; the state of being unified as a continent.

ALTRUISTIM: the belief or practice of kindness and selfless concern for the wellbeing of others.

DECKS ARE STACKED: a situation or condition in which an unfavorable outcome is overwhelmingly unlikely.

DISPERSAL: action or purpose of distributing people or things over a wide area.

ENCLAVE: a portion of a territory; in this case, it is a portion of Africa surrounded by other African territories, which Africans has been made to believe are different from each other because of nationality.

EXTRA-AFRRICAN NATIONS: outside of Africa, or beyond Africa. Non-African nations.

LALA –LAND: a fanciful state of dreamland.

HUNKY-DORY: American slang, meaning all will be fine.

HAKUNA MATATA: no problem, don't worry; a nonchalant attitude toward life.

LIQUID GOLD/BLACK GOLD: oil or petroleum.

MARSHAL PLAN: program of financial aid and other aid, massive economic assistant given to Europe and Japan post world war two.

MISNOMER: inaccurate name or designation.

NITROGLYCERIN: an explosive, a very unstable explosive.

OOMPH: informal word for exciting, energetic, the extra drive, the extra push above normal.

PASS MUSTER: be accepted as adequate or satisfactory.

POTENTIATION: to increase the power, the strength, the effect, or likelihood of something.

SNAKE OIL: slang for a substance of no medicinal value, sold as a remedy for all disease.

SPIGOT: a tap or device that controls the flow of liquid; in this case, a device that controls the flow of ideas.

UMPTEEN: indefinitely many.

VESTIGIAL: part of the body that, over the course of time, becomes atrophied or degenerated. Also a remnant of something that was once much larger or more noticeable.

REFERENCES

H.J. de belij, peter muller 2003
Berlin confrence document. Geography, realms, regions and concepts

John Wiley and son inc, oct 2005
www.homestead.com/wysinger/berlinconference.html

prof Ali Mazrui
Nkrumahism and the triple heritage; out of the shadows
Third lecture aggrey -fraser-guggisberg memorial lectures, University of Ghana, Legon, Accra 2002
www.igcs.binghamton.edu/igcs_site/dirton17.htm

Gerald Mwale
Civil society organizations slam Africa's poor health records
Millennium campaign
www.millenniumcampaign.org

Armed forces of the world
Diversity Inc Magazine
www.strategypage.com/fyeo/hoetomakewar/databases/armies/a.asp

Jeffrey Donovan
Poland: Solidarity-The trade union that change the world
Radio liberty-Radio freė Europe
www.rferl.org/featurearticle/2005/08

Cora Agatucci
Part II African Empires
AD/CE 1ST-15TH Centuries
www.cocc.edu

The Great Wall of China
William Edgar Geil
Sturgis and Walton Company 1909
Harvard University Library

Made in the USA
Monee, IL
05 November 2026

67381752R00092